# A Season of
# Nature Poems for
# Catholic Children

## Winter

# A Winter Season of Nature Poems for Catholic Children

Janet P. McKenzie, OCDS

A Race for Heaven Book

Biblio Resource Publications, Inc.
108½ S. Moore St.
Bessemer, MI 49911
2020

## Other Books in the Nature Poems for Catholic Children Series

*A  Spring Season of Nature Poems
for Catholic Children*

*A Summer Season of Nature Poems
for Catholic Children*

*An Autumn Season of Nature Poems
for Catholic Children*

# OTHER BOOKS BY JANET P. MCKENZIE
## WWW.RACEFORHEAVEN.COM

### STUDY GUIDES AND AIDS

✝ A Series of 20 Saint Study Guides for the saint books written by Mary Fabyan Windeatt (available as individual study guides or grade-level guides)

✝ *Graced Encounters with Mary Fabyan Windeatt's Saints: 344 Ways to Imitate the Holy Habits of Saints*

✝ *The Windeatt Dictionary: Pre-Vatican II Terms and Catholic Words from Mary Fabyan Windeatt's Saint Biographies*

✝ *Reading the Saints: Lists of Catholic Books for Children plus Book Collecting Tips for the Home and School Library, Second Edition*

✝ *Alternative Books Reports for Catholic Students*

✝ *The King of the Golden City Study Edition* (includes text and guide or individual guide available)

✝ *Outlaws of Ravenhurst Study Edition* (includes text and guide or individual guide available)

✝ *The Family that Overtook Christ Study Edition: Lessons in Sanctity from the Family of St. Bernard of Clairvaux* (includes text and guide)

✝ *By Cross and Anchor Study Edition: The Story of Frederic Baraga on Lake Superior* (includes text and guide)

### RECONCILIATION/FIRST HOLY COMMUNION

✝ *A Reconciliation Reader-Retreat: Read-aloud Lessons, Stories, and Poems for Young Catholics Preparing for Confession*

- *Communion with the Saints, A Family Preparation Program for First Communion and Beyond in the Spirit of St. Therese*
- *The King of the Golden City Study Edition* (includes text and guide or individual guide available)
- *My First Communion Journal in Imitation of St. Therese, the Little Flower*
- *My First Communion Journal in Imitation of St. Paul: Putting on the Armor of God*
- *The Good Shepherd and His Little Lambs Study Edition: A First Communion Story-Primer*

## SACRAMENT OF CONFIRMATION

- *A Confirmation Reader-Retreat: Read-Aloud Lessons, Stories, and Poems for Young Catholics*
- *The Family that Overtook Christ Study Edition: Lessons in Sanctity from the Family of St. Bernard of Clairvaux* (adult and older teens)

## ST. JOSEPH

- *The Month of St. Joseph: Prayers and Practices for Each Day of March in Imitation of the Virtues of St. Joseph* (adult and older teens)
- *Devotion to St. Joseph: Read-Aloud Stories, Poems, and Prayers for Catholic Children*

## OTHER BOOKS

- *I Talk with God: The Art of Prayer and Meditation for Catholic Children*
- *Bedtime Bible Stories for Catholic Children: Loving Jesus through His Word*

This book is dedicated to my grandchildren: Ali, Grace, Norah, Ethan, Katie, Jon, Jacob, Elena, and all those to come.

Nature is so much more fun and inspiring when I explore it with you.

With great love,
Nana

# Acknowledgements

Dust Jacket Design by Joshua Kodis

Dust Jacket Photo ©bgfoto iStockPhoto.com

Dust Jacket Graphic ©Yevhenii Dubinko
iStockPhoto.com

Divider Page Illustration ©Ievgeniia Lytvynovych
iStockPhoto.com

Illustrations on December 4, December 19,
February 4, and February 7
©Mellok iStockPhoto,com

Illustration on January 4 ©FrankRmspott
IStockPhoto.com

Illustration on January 16 ©Dn Br
Shutterstock.com

Illustration on January 24 ©alexblacksea
Shutterstock.com

"The Baptism: Matthew 3:1-17" and "An
Unplanned Child" © 2019 Janet P. McKenzie

But now ask the beasts to teach you,
the birds of the air to tell you;
Or speak to the earth to instruct you,
and the fish of the sea to inform you.
Which of all these does not know
that the hand of God has done this?

Job 12:7-9

And Nature, the old nurse, took
The child upon her knee,
Saying: "Here is a story-book
thy Father has written for thee."

"Come, wander with me," she said,
"Into regions yet untrod;
And read what is still unread
In the manuscripts of God."

And he wandered away and away
With Nature, the dear old nurse,
Who sang to him night and day
The rhymes of the universe.

From "The Fiftieth Birthday of Agassiz" by
Henry Wadsworth Longfellow (1807-1882)

# TABLE OF CONTENTS

# PREFACE

Throughout my childhood, my father worked as a manager in the Michigan State Parks system. We moved every three or four years to a different park within Michigan's Upper Peninsula. Even as a young child, I remember spending long days and evenings outdoors—in the woods, on the beach, in the yard. Many of these memories include my siblings and neighborhood friends. But many are the times I spent alone at various "secret" places I had found, places I often escaped to in order to think deep-child thoughts—to communicate with God.

Although I hesitate to compare my experiences with those of a saint, St. Thérèse the Little Flower, describes similar experiences in *The Story of a Soul*: "I preferred to go *alone* and sit down on the grass bedecked with flowers, and then my thoughts became very profound indeed! Without knowing what it was to meditate, my soul was absorbed in real prayer" (SOS 37). St. Thérèse talks often of how she was inspired to love, praise, and understand the God that the book of nature opened to her.

As a Discalced Carmelite Secular, my life is focused on union with God. Like St. Augustine (yes, another saint comparison!), I searched for many years for God, in various places and circumstances. However, in my Carmelite journey of faith, I have discovered that God can be found within. He resides in our very souls—nearer to us than we are to ourselves. Yet, in my adult searching, I have found —just as in my childhood—that I often commune best with Him in natural environments. I feel His presence in the beauty and holy silence of nature. Surrounded by creation, my mind frees, my soul fills with gratitude, and my heart connects with our loving Creator.

Here too we are in good company with the saints. Both St. Teresa of Jesus and St. John of the Cross, Carmelite Doctors, often used the natural world as a conduit to God:

✞ "It helped me also to look at fields, or water, or flowers. In these things I found a remembrance of the creator. I mean that they awakened and recollected me and served as a book and reminded me of my ingratitude and sins" (St. Teresa of Jesus, *Life* 9.5).

✞ "Beholding in creation a trace of the divine beauty, power, and loving wisdom, John could not easily resist the enchantment of nature. . . . He would take the friars out to the mountains . . . so that each might pass the day alone there 'in solitary prayer'" (*The Collected Works of St. John of the Cross* 26).

Many are the quotations we could cite from saints, popes, theologians, the Catechism, and Scripture that support an appreciation of the natural world as an important dimension of our relationship with God. However, we also need an awareness of the errors of the "New Age" movement, the theological problems with "nature worship", the heresy of pantheism, and an understanding that God does not depend upon creation for His identity to direct our path. If you are concerned or curious about these issues, please review the Appendix of this book.

In this series, we embark upon a study of nature and God in nature by reading aloud one poem per day, spending time daily outdoors, and, like St. Thérèse, thinking about God. I believe that the beauty, the rhythm, the flow, and the openness of poetry lends itself particularly useful as we journey closer to God with our beloved children and grandchildren in union with what Pope Frances calls "the joyful mystery of God" in creation. May God bless you!

16 July, 2019, Feast of Our Lady of Mount Carmel

# A Few Explanations and Suggestions

## The Purpose of This Study

The purpose of this poetical study of nature through the seasons is two-fold:

1) To seek and experience God personally and intimately by daily exposure to His creative work in nature

2) To better appreciate the connection between all of God's creation, its meaning and value, and its role—and ours—in the harmonious praise of God

Briefly, each creation of God has its own value and significance as well as a unique nature that is dependent on the rest of creation. Each creature works to complete and serve the rest of creation. (See *CCC* ¶340.) All of creation's natures, working together as a system of natures, are what we call "nature"—which "can only be understood as a gift from the outstretched hand of the Father of all" (*Laudato Si'* ¶76). The purpose of all of God's creation—including us—is to give Him praise and glory: ". . . so that we might exist for the praise of his glory . . ." (Ephesians 1:12).

Our study of God's creation through poetry and outdoor exploration is intended to allow children—and their adult companions—to experience God in a different way, to see Him in a new light, and to deepen our relationship and appreciation for Him and all of His creation—to learn to pray and praise God continuously. This is not a new way of experiencing God. Check out the Psalms and other books of the Bible. Refer to the writings of St. Thomas

Aquinas and many other saints. Peruse the teachings of our last three popes—St. Pope John Paul II, Pope Benedict XVI, and Pope Francis. Read through the *Catechism of the Catholic Church*, which clearly states: "There is a solidarity among all creatures arising from the fact that all have the same Creator and are all ordered to his glory . . ." (344). (For a more thorough treatment of seeking God through nature in accordance with the teachings of the Catholic Church, please see the Appendix of this book.)

Hopefully, through the gentle art of poetry and a daily commitment to experience God's creation outdoors, our relationship with God will become more awestruck as it becomes filled with the wonder, love, and appreciation of His divine wisdom and loving providence. God is more than willing to meet us whenever we reach out to Him. A little bit of openness and availability on our part will go a long way toward helping us fulfill our mission to praise God's glory in all our being. Let us begin today.

# HOW THIS STUDY IS ORGANIZED

## ASTRONOMICAL VS. METEOROLOGICAL SEASONS

Astronomical seasons are based on where the sun is in relation to the Earth, with the equinoxes (March and September) marking the dates where the day-to-night ratio is exactly twelve hours each. Because the Earth does not take exactly 365 days to travel around the sun, these dates vary but are generally considered to be March 21 and September 22 with the solstices usually falling on June 21 and December 22—the days with the longest and shortest periods of daylight. So the first day of each season according to the astronomical calendar would correspond to the varying dates of the spring and fall equinoxes and the summer and winter solstices.

The meteorological calendar for seasons uses the more general three-month chunk of time that is most closely associated with that season's weather. This calendar has the following seasonal dates:

- Winter: December 1 to February 28 or 29
- Spring: March 1 to May 31
- Summer: June 1 to August 31, and
- Autumn: September 1 to November 30

As the meteorological seasonal calendar corresponds more closely with our liturgical year, which begins in the season of Advent around December 1, (and breaks the months of each season more cleanly), this poetical study of the seasons uses the meteorological calendar to track the seasons.

(Please note that much of the material in this study is geared toward the weather and activities common to the temperate climates. My personal experience is almost exclusively that of the upper Midwest of the United States. Adaptation may be necessary depending on your location.)

## LITURGICAL VS. NATURAL YEAR
Traditionally, we Americans often begin new projects and make new resolutions at the beginning of our Gregorian calendar year on January 1. Our Church's Roman Rite liturgical new year always begins on the first Sunday of Advent. This date is determined by when the Sunday closest to the Feast of St. Andrew (November 30) falls. The earliest this date can be is November 27, and the latest possible date is December 3. The beginning of the winter season of this series would roughly correspond with the beginning of the Church's liturgical new year.

The other major season of the liturgical year is the season of Lent, which is generally associated with the natural

3

season of spring. As the timing of this season depends on the moveable feast day of Easter, Ash Wednesday, the first day of Lent, may be as early as February 4 or as late as March 10, with the date of Easter itself ranging from March 22 to April 25. Therefore, the Lenten season is covered in this study in both the winter and spring seasons.

## WHEN AND HOW TO START

There is no "right" starting place for this series—no "correct" season to begin this poetical study of God's creation. Many may wish to start with the Church's new liturgical year in December—the winter season. However, feel free to start with the season that best suits your own calendar and availability. Perhaps summer, when school is in recess and life is more laid back, is a better fit for your schedule. Quite possibly, autumn— the beginning of the school year—appeals to you as the best time to start. Maybe you want to examine the optional theme for each season and choose to begin according to which theme seems most interesting to you and your family.

Whenever you begin, remember the program's two main rules:

1.  Read one poem daily *aloud* and have a short discussion on it. (Suggestions for age-appropriate questions can be found below.)
2.  Spend at least thirty minutes each and every day outdoors, exploring God's beautiful creative work. This includes you as well as the children. Always keep in mind that the best way to get children outdoors is to go with them. Trust me; you will be enriched beyond your expectations. Do not hesitate to assume the role of nature mentor to help

4

your children or grandchildren increase their love of nature and deepen their experience of God. Review the section on nature mentoring if you need the reassurance that no prior experience or knowledge is necessary. You—yes, you—can do this!

# THE DAILY ROUTINE

## THE POEMS – DAILY AND SUPPLEMENTAL

For each day of the year, a poem (or several shorter poems) is presented for reading. The poem may be about an aspect of nature for that season, relate to the seasonal theme, or to a specific activity common for that season. Read each poem aloud. Perhaps each child could also read the poem aloud. Read slowly and with feeling. Don't hesitate to re-read the poem several times. If a child takes a special liking to a poem, help the child to memorize it. Having three or four favorite poems in a memory bank provides a store of great pleasure that will bubble up and spill out on days when our love of nature overwhelms us and we have no other way to express our joy in that special experience. It is a great treasure.

In addition to the daily poems, several other poems are available in the supplemental poetry section following the daily poems. These poems focus on the liturgical year or specific national holidays. They may be chosen to read aloud instead of, or in addition to, the poem for each day. There is a poem available for each day of Christmas, each day of Lent, and at least one poem for each significant holiday or Catholic holy day. Additionally, there are poems for meditation upon the themes for the First Friday and First Saturday devotions. Use the supplemental poems as you deem best for your family—either replacing the daily poem, read in addition to the daily poem, or not read at all. If you wish to incorporate them into the daily routine, it may require some preparation time to preview these poems to determine which ones best suit your family and purposes. Be sure to discuss these poems with the children/grandchildren just as you would the daily poems.

As you and your family begin to read more and more poetry, be sure to note favorite poets. Go online and check out more poems by these favorites or perhaps purchase as a gift an entire volume written by them. Pay attention to the type of poetry (rhythm and rhyme scheme) that appeals to each child. Encourage them to take a favorite poem, study how it is written, and use it as a pattern for writing an original poem of their own. Perhaps after reading a poem, they may decide that they could write a better poem on that topic. The world needs poetry and poets; coax the young poets around you to produce poetry that they enjoy writing and sharing. Model writing poetry by generating poems of your own.

## DISCUSSION

To encourage discussion, always ask open-ended questions that require more than a yes/no answer. For younger children, the following questions offer a good beginning but remember that not all questions will apply to every poem. As you gain confidence, feel free to construct your own questions geared toward the ages and interests of your own children/grandchildren.

1. What is this poem about?
2. How does this poem make you feel?
3. What action do you want to take because of this poem?
4. What did you learn from this poem?
5. What does this poem suggest about God?

A different approach is to ask each child to retell the poem in their own words, starting with the youngest child and having each child add something to the re-telling. (Educator Charlotte Mason calls this technique "narration.")

For older children (and adults), try using the following three principles/realities/values that stem from the teachings of Thomas Berry, Catholic eco-theologian and author of several books including *The Dream of the Earth* and *The Great Work: Our Way into the Future.* According to Thomas Berry, these three characteristics govern the universe and reveal what the universe has to teach us. (These questions are also appropriate to ask as a nature mentor when outside exploring nature with children.)

1. Uniqueness (Each creation offers a unique expression of the divine, an authenticity that illustrates how the divine image dwells within.)
   - How is this creation different from all others? What makes it unique?
   - How does it reveal the divine?

2. Interior Identity
   - What is the job or specific task of this creation?
   - How does it function?
   - How does it give harmonious praise to God?

3. Communion/Connection
   - What is the relationship between this creation and the rest of creation?
   - How does it serve or provide for the rest of creation?
   - How is it connected to or dependent upon the rest of creation?

## The Quotations

The quotations beneath the daily poems are included for the adults participating in this study. Often, as we feed our children the knowledge and inspiration they crave and need, our own needs may go unfulfilled. These short selections are intended to inspire you, deepen your understanding about an idea or topic, or add a touch of humor.

## Additional Resources

This section first includes appropriate picture books for children. In preparation for this section, hundreds of possibly worthy picture books were read and examined; many of these books were discarded in favor of the exceptional books chosen for each season. The books marked "Stellar" would be considered "must reads" for each season. The remaining books have been categorized according to the holidays and optional themes for each season. The intention is that these books would be read aloud by either an adult or child.

Depending on the interests of your children/grandchildren, you may wish to focus on one particular theme or perhaps choose several books from each category. (It would be hard to read them all!) As you read through these books, be sure to note the author of those books you particularly enjoy. Watch for other books by these authors listed in this series, and/or check them out at your local library.

After the final section of picture books, there is a short section on other nature books for children. This section varies with the season and is outlined below.

Winter: Nature Non-fiction Books for Children
Spring: A Short List of Children's Nature Authors

Summer: A Short List of Children's Nature Poets, Collectable Children's Poetry Books, and A Few Children's Poetry Anthologies

Fall: A Short List of Children's Nature Chapter Books

The last part of this section contains recommended adult books that fall loosely in the following categories:
- The "Why" of Nature
- Connection with Nature
- Nature Activity Books—Outdoor Adventuring
- Nature Journaling
- Nature Crafts and Drawing Books
- Nature Books for Grandparents
- The Practice of *Shinrin-yoku:* Forest Therapy or Forest Bathing
- The Practice of Mindfulness

## OUTSIDE ACTIVITY

The crux and primary purpose of this poetry series is to explore nature and to seek God in His beautiful creation. If you are unsure about what to do outside, check out the "Additional Resources" section described above for ideas. Assume your role as nature mentor as described on pages 17-21 below.

By spending unfettered time in nature, we will unleash our sense of wonder and come to better understand God. By increasing our familiarity with different aspects of nature, we will begin to see the connection between all creation and discover the loving concern God has for us all.

Please make the effort to get your family (including yourself!) outside for least thirty minutes each day—an hour would not be too much! Get outside, play, experience creation, and live in the present moment. Be sure to pause occasionally in holy silence to give thanks, glory, and praise to our awesome Creator!

## OPTIONAL SEASONAL THEMES

For those interested in a more guided study of nature, each season has a theme of recommended focus. These themes provide a hub around which outside activity for each season can be centered as well as an emphasis on specific knowledge and experience of God's created world.

Do not get obsessive with the suggested resources below. Choose only those best suited to your particular situation. Be flexible. Taylor these suggestions to your own circumstances and time allowances.

WINTER THEME: Reflecting on the Mystery of God through Natural Prayer

- DEFINITION OF NATURAL PRAYER: Finding intimacy with God by experiencing Him in the beauty of nature; prayer experienced amidst creation (Beware, however, of the caution expressed by St. John of the Cross in *Ascent of Mount Carmel* 3.24.4: If the heart and soul are not elevated to God, an experience of sensory delight may merely be another form of recreation.)

- GOAL: Mystic—someone who seeks union with God through prayer and self-surrender

- SUMMARY: The season of winter—when much of nature is at rest and we anticipate and contemplate the Mystery of God in the Christ Child—is a great time to reconnect with that wonder for God that natural experiences (a beautiful sunset, a snowy-topped mountain, a perfect snowflake) so easily enkindle. Enjoy the stillness of winter while practicing the virtue of holy silence—quiet walks in the snow, a pause to listen to the winter birds. Take your daily prayer time (rosary or meditation) outside. "We need to find God, and he cannot be found in noise and restlessness. God is the friend of silence. See how nature—trees, flowers, grass—grows in silence; see the stars, the moon and the sun, how they move in silence . . ." (St. Teresa of Calcutta).

- ADULT RESOURCES
  - *Natural Prayer: Encountering God in Nature* by Wayne Simsic
  - *The Secret Life of John Paul II* by Lino Zani
  - *When the Trees Say Nothing* by Thomas Merton

- CHILDREN'S RESOURCES
  - *A Quiet Place* by Douglas Wood
  - *Crinkleroot's Book of Animal Tracking* by Jim Arnosky
  - *The Other Way to Listen* by Byrd Baylor
  - *The Wild Weather Book* by Fiona Danks and Jo Schofield
  - *WoodsWalk* by Henry W. Art and Michael W. Robbins

SPRING THEME: Detecting God in Nature through Phenology

- DEFINITION OF PHENOLOGY: Nature's calendar; nature's clock; the study of the timing of seasonal biological activities including first flowers, leaf budding, bird migration, etc. (We can also include *seasonality*, which is the study of changes in the physical environment such as first frost, date the ice melts, etc.)

- GOAL: Nature Detective—someone who carefully observes the wonders and mystery of nature

A Few Explanations and Suggestions

- SUMMARY: Spend spring observing firsts and lasts in nature: first robin, first eruptions of various plants and flowers, first sound of the frog voices, last frost, last ice on the lake. Mark these dates on a regular or perpetual calendar—an excellent beginning toward keeping a more complete nature journal. Allow the children free rein to explore and take notes and photos of various aspects of God's creation. "Nature is a constant source of wonder and awe" (Pope Francis, *Laudato Si'* 85).

- ADULT RESOURCES
  - 📖 Daily readings from any of the following: *Hal Borland's Book of Days* (New England), *A Walk through the Year* by Edwin Way Teale (New England), or *Wit & Wisdom of the Great Outdoors* by Larry Wilber (upper Midwest)
  - 📖 **Or** weekly readings from *The Beginning Naturalist* by Gale Lawrence or shorter articles for each month in *A Seasonal Guide to the Natural Year* by John Bates (upper Midwest), or *Minnesota Phenology* by Larry Weber
  - 📖 **Or** browse through any calendar/almanac suited to your location.
  - 📖 Check into joining a citizen science program of interest.

- CHILDREN'S RESOURCES
  - 📖 *Crinkleroot's Nature Almanac* by Jim Arnosky
  - 📖 *One Day in the Woods* by Jean Craighead George
  - 📖 *This World of Wonder* by Hal Borland
  - 📖 *When I Consider* by Marian M. Schoolland

SUMMER THEME: Inspecting God's Glorious Creation through Naming Nature (Nomenclature)

- DEFINITION OF NOMENCLATURE: A system of names in a given field such as botany or biology

- GOAL: Naturalist—someone who is an expert or student in the study of plants, animals, and the natural world

- SUMMARY: By taking an interest in nature and being willing to make the acquaintance of the most common natural elements in your locale—by learning the names of the most common birds, flowers, and trees—we can become more acquainted with all that surrounds us in God's great outdoors. Names foster familiarity, and lead to a sense of connection. "What I know of the divine sciences and the Holy Scriptures, I have learned in woods and fields. I have no other masters than the beeches and the oaks" (St. Bernard of Clairvaux).

- ADULT RESOURCES
  - 📖 *Beyond Your Doorstep* by Hal Borland
  - 📖 *Circle of the Seasons* by Edwin Way Teale
  - 📖 *Exploring Nature with Your Child* by Dorothy Edwards Shuttlesworth
  - 📖 *Great Lakes Nature* by Mary Blocksma
  - 📖 *Handbook of Nature Study* by Anna Botsford Comstock [a classic since 1939]
  - 📖 *The Naturalist's Notebook* by Nathaniel T. Wheelwright and Bernd Heinrich

- CHILDREN'S RESOURCES
  - 📖 Regional field guides (the more specific to your area the better) to birds, flowers, insects, trees, or any other area of interest

13

📖 *Nature Anatomy* by Julia Rothman

📖 Any of the *True Books* (*True Book of Insects*, etc.) published by Children's Press in the 1950's and 1960's

📖 Any of Jim Arnosky's *Crinkleroot's Guide to Knowing* books (*Birds, Trees*, etc.)

📖 *Crinkleroot's Guide to Walking in Wild Places*

AUTUMN THEME: Respecting God's Creation through Care of the Natural World

- GOAL: Eco-Catholic

- DEFINITION OF ECO-CATHOLIC: Someone who values not only Catholic spirituality and doctrine but also the natural world, the environment, and justice

- SUMMARY: In his 2015 encyclical *Laudato Si'*, Pope Francis encourages "every person living on this planet" to take better care of our common home, Earth. Like his three predecessors, he emphasizes the need to care for and understand the connection between all of God's creation. Review carefully your family's relationship with the natural world and the habits that support the environment and those that are detrimental. "Care for the environment represents a challenge for all of humanity. It is a matter of a common and universal duty, that of respecting a common good" (Pope St. John Paul II, *Centesimus Annus*, 40).

- ADULT RESOURCES
  📖 *Caring for Creation in Your Own Backyard: Over 100 Things Christian Families Can Do to Help the Earth (A Seasonal Guide)* by Loren & Mary Ruth Wilkinson

14

- 📖 *Earthsongs: Praying with Nature* by Wayne Simsic
- 📖 *In Defense of Nature* by Benjamin Wiker
- 📖 *Laudato Si'* by Pope Francis
- 📖 *Life from Our Land* by Marcus Grodi
- 📖 *The Joyful Mystery: Field Notes toward a Green Thomism* by Christopher J. Thompson

- CHILDREN'S RESOURCES
  - 📖 *Celebrate the Earth: Psalm 104* by Dorrie Papademetriou
  - 📖 *Crinkleroot's Guide to Giving Back to Nature* by Jim Arnosky
  - 📖 *Song of Francis* by Tomie dePaola
  - 📖 Read and implement actions proposed by Pope Francis in ¶211 of *Laudato Si'*.

---

Note that these suggested themes are *optional*. If the children are young, or if the themes seem intimidating to implement, feel free to skip them. Perhaps you would like to utilize the picture books as your only use of the optional season themes. Or maybe you would like to study the suggested adult resources for your own enrichment without adding the children's resources.

Be kind to yourself. We're going for joy here—not added stress! Do not put pressure to use every resource and/or theme. Attach no guilt to customizing and simplifying. The main objective is to enjoy God's creation and to connect with the Creator—not to cram in every possible teaching moment. Allow the children to ask and find answers to their own spontaneous questions in an adventure of discovery at their own lead. Relax and enjoy!

"FOR FROM THE GREATNESS
AND THE BEAUTY OF CREATED THINGS
THEIR ORIGINAL AUTHOR,
BY ANALOGY,
IS SEEN."

WISDOM 13:5

## You Can Become a Nature Mentor (Almost Without Trying)

"If a child is to keep alive his inborn sense of wonder . . . he needs the companionship of at least one adult who can share it, rediscovering with him the joy, excitement, and mystery of the world we live in" (Rachel Carson in *A Sense of Wonder*). This "one adult" becomes this child's nature mentor. It is not a difficult task. It does not require vast knowledge. According to Rachel Carson, it is based upon "having fun together rather than teaching." Whether you are a grandparent, a parent, a teacher, the neighbor down the street, or an aunt like Rachel Carson, you need no advance preparation other than asking yourself, "Am I up for adventure?" "Can I handle being a co-conspirator?"

The best nature mentors are not those who have the answers but who can stimulate the questions, who can step aside and let the child take charge. Effective nature mentors are those who are fellow adventurers, willing to let their own sense of wonder come alive, and share their feelings about nature—and reverence for nature—rather than merely providing explanations and facts. Observe and explore. Be aware and listen—not only to the wonders around you but to those sharing the experience with you. Be respectful to the child's interests and enthusiasms. Be attentive to the present moment—the activity and the feelings that are evoked.

Ask questions. Point out interesting sights, sounds, animals, and plants. Bring home specimens to talk about, learn about, and display. Include God in the discussion.

Help them to observe the activity around them. Allow them to directly experience the wonder that surrounds them —saving the "teaching moment" for a later recap of the event. Encourage them to see, hear, smell, and touch. Allow them not only to run and enjoy but also to sit in holy silence and observe—watch the grass bending in the wind, hear the babble of nearby water and birds, smell the flowers and the bark of the trees, touch the moss and slippery rocks—pondering and raising the heart to God. The love of nature is best inspired by experiencing nature —even quiet observation can be an interactive encounter on an emotional level.

Be enthusiastic and joyful in all their discoveries. Play games; join in their fun. Often, the memory of an experience is associated with the emotions related to that experience. By making time with nature joy-filled, joy will come to be an emotion associated with nature itself.

Sharing the natural world with others adds to the richness of the encounter—not only at the moment but later in discussion. Take time each day to reflect together on time spent in nature, reviewing individual discoveries and emotions. In this way, everyone benefits from each person's experience and insights, and our own encounters become more meaningful. Additionally, a bit of nature bonding and affirmation occurs that binds us with each other, and more deeply with the created world.

As a nature mentor, basic knowledge may be helpful but, in this case, only a little knowledge of nature is not a dangerous thing—or even detrimental. Enjoyment of simple natural aspects (the colors of the sunset, the blowing clouds, the calls of birds, the vastness of the night sky, the feel of rain on your face) will serve to enkindle more joy and wonder than many interesting facts. "I sincerely believe that for the child, and for the parent seeking to guide him, it is not half so important to know as to feel" (Rachel Carson).

It is more helpful to arouse their curiosity and sense of wonder than to pepper them with facts and names they may or may not be able to assimilate. As a nature mentor, receptivity and awareness trump personal resources. Is it less wondrous to gaze at the night sky even if you do not know the name of a single star or constellation?

Encourage exploration using the senses of smell and hearing. This is particularly effective at night and in rainy weather. The smell of the ocean, frog ponds, and rain-filled forests can provide lasting memories. The night sound of insects, frogs, flight of birds overhead, thunder, and wind are especially powerful. Try to focus not only on the full chorus of sound but also on each of the individual contributors. Seek where they are hiding.

Unfortunately, it is easy to become immune to the wonder of God's creation—to become insensitive to repeated exposure to God's great gifts. Rachel Carson would have us ask, "What if I had never seen this before? What if I knew I would never see it again?" Like the reception of Holy Communion, when we take for granted that we can receive It often, we often receive It less (and less reverently). The same holds true of God's gifts within the natural world. Because we can see it all the time, we often see (and enjoy its benefits) less often. When is the last time you took the time to explore the night sky? Or pause your busy agenda to enjoy the glorious sunset? Or listen attentively for even a minute or two to the morning chorus of birds? Learn to tune in to God not only in church, but also in His cathedral of the natural world.

## RESOURCES

So what resources are required to be an effective nature mentor? For starters, you may want to read one or more of the books that most directly influenced the above insights and ideas:

&#x1F4D6; *The Sense of Wonder* by Rachel Carson (1956)

&#x1F4D6; *Sharing Nature with Children: The Classic Parents' and Teachers' Nature Awareness Guidebook* by Joseph Cornell (1979—a newer edition is available)

&#x1F4D6; *How to Raise a Wild Child: The Art and Science of Falling in Love with Nature* by Scott D. Sampson (2015)

Spending a few dollars on a good magnifying glass or hands lens will pay off handsomely. With this, a snow-flake or grain of sand takes on far greater wonder as does a drop of pond water or the moon at night. You may wish to throw down another couple of dollars on child-sized flashlights—or ultraviolet flashlights!—for night exploration of insects, rocks, and flowers. (Bedtime can wait!)

As far as expensive equipment and toys, do not let your heart be troubled. In 2012, *Wired* magazine published an article entitled "The 5 Best Toys of All Time." Here is your shopping list:

1. Stick
2. Box
3. String
4. Cardboard Tube
5. Dirt

If you must spend money, a few good field guides may be helpful—the more regional the better—for identifi-ication of common trees, birds, flowers, and insects. Keep in mind, however, this caution from Rachel Carson: "I think the value of the game of identification depends on how you play it. If it becomes an end in itself, I count it of little use. It is possible to compile extensive lists of creatures seen and identified without ever once having caught a breath-taking glimpse of the wonder of life. If a child asked me a question that suggested even a faint awareness of the mystery behind the arrival of a migrant sandpiper on the beach of an August morning, I would be far more pleased than by the mere fact that he knew it was a sandpiper and not a plover."

A pair of puddle boots, some old clothes, and raingear (purchased or makeshift) will allow your child to explore without fear of "getting dirty." Be sure to provide the same for yourself.

Nature mentoring really is as simple as accompanying kids outside and letting them do what comes naturally. Let them be the boss. If you are doubtful, try at least a half-hour outside every day for a month—put it on your calendar. While Scott Sampson in *How to Raise a Wild Child* claims, "The best place to fall in love with nature is wherever you happen to be," be sure to vary the setting occasionally. Find a place where you (as well as the children) are excited to be. See what effect this daily thirty-minute habit has—on you and the kids!

Rachel Carson had one wish for every child: ". . . a sense of wonder so indestructible that it would last throughout life, as an unfailing antidote against the boredom and disenchantments of later years, the sterile preoccupation with things that are artificial, the alienation from the sources of our strength." It is in wonder that we often find God.

"... HE FIXED THE ORDERED SEASONS
AND THE BOUNDARIES OF
THEIR REGIONS,
SO THAT PEOPLE MIGHT SEEK GOD,
EVEN PERHAPS GROPE FOR HIM
AND FIND HIM,
THOUGH INDEED HE IS NOT FAR
FROM ANY ONE OF US."

ACTS 17:26-27

# DECEMBER

### THE QUEEN OF THE YEAR
Edna Dean Proctor (1829-1923), published in
*Poems*, 1890

WHEN suns are low, and nights are long,
    And winds bring wild alarms,
Through the darkness comes the queen of the year
    In all her peerless charms,—
December, fair and holly-crowned,
    With the Christ-child in her arms.

The maiden months are a stately train—
    Veiled in the spotless snow,
Or decked with the bloom of Paradise
    What time the roses blow,
Or wreathed with the vine and the yellow wheat
    When the noons of harvest glow.

But O the joy of the rolling year,
    The queen with peerless charms,
Is she who comes through the waning light
    To keep the world from harms,—
December, fair and holly-crowned,
    With the Christ-child in her arms.

> "AND MARY KEPT ALL THESE THINGS,
> REFLECTING ON THEM IN HER HEART. "
> LUKE 2:19

## HIS MOTHER'S INVITATION

S. Marr, published in *"Ave Maria"* magazine,
December 4, 1909

When Advent shadows seem to bring
　　The feast of Christmas near,
We should our Blessed Mother's voice
　　In loving accents hear.

It is as if our gentle Queen
　　Invited every one
To gather at the Bethlehem Crib
　　In honor of her Son.

She asks us all for Christmas Day,
　　Reminding us to bring
A little gift to mark the feast,
　　The birthday of the King.

And so we have the Advent weeks
　　That we may ready be
To bring unto the Crib our gifts
　　For Mary's Son to see.

His Mother says the gift that will
　　The greatest joy impart,
In honor of the birthday feast,
　　Is just a loving heart.

So let us get them ready now,
　　That, when the carols ring,
We all may have a birthday gift
　　In honor of the King.

"No one has ever seen God. Yet, if we love one
another, God remains in us, and his love is brought to
perfection in us." – 1 John 4:12

## THE STAR
Jane Taylor (1783-1824), published in
*Rhymes for the Nursery*, 1824

'Twinkle, twinkle, little star,
How I wonder what you are!
Up above the world so high,
Like a diamond in the sky.

When the blazing sun is gone,
When he nothing shines upon,
Then you show your little light,
Twinkle, twinkle, all the night.

Then the trav'ller in the dark,
Thanks you for your tiny spark,
He could not see which way to go,
If you did not twinkle so.

In the dark blue sky you keep,
And often through my curtains peep,
For you never shut your eye
Till the sun is in the sky.

As your bright and tiny spark,
Lights the trav'ller in the dark,
Though I know not what you are,
Twinkle, twinkle, little star.

"If the stars should appear one night in a thousand
years, how men would believe and adore; and
preserve for many generations the remembrance of
the City of God which has been shown."
Ralph Waldo Emerson

## A LESSON FROM THE SNOWFLAKES
Sister Mary Josita Belger (1899-1978), published in
*Sing a Song of Holy Things*, 1945

The grass and flowers have gone to sleep
　In warm, dark earthy beds.
And now God sends His snowflakes down
　To cover up their heads.

The little starry snowflakes
　Come flying, flying down
And make a soft white blanket
　Over all the town.

My soul will be that lovely
　If I keep it pure and bright,
Always following my angel,
　Always trying to do right.

"Announced by all the trumpets of the sky,
arrives the snow." – Ralph Waldo Emerson

### OUTSIDE THE DOOR
Annette Wynne (died 1953), published in
*For Days and Days*, 1919

O utside the door the bare tree stands,

And catches snowflakes in its hands,
And holds them well and holds them high,
Until a puffing wind comes by.

"'The folk wisdom about the forest being more than
just a collection of trees is, indeed, a first working
principle of ecology.'" – Christopher J Thompson, *In
Defense of Nature, quoting Odum and Barrett*

## THE ALL ALONE TREE
F. O'Neill Gallagher, published in *Everychild*, 1921

There's a tree that is growing alone on the hill,
By the path that winds up at the back of the mill,
And we're awfully fond of it, Maudie and me,
And we call it the All Alone, All Alone Tree.

It is old, and it's wrinkled and twisted and dry
And it grows by itself with no other tree nigh,
And we always sit under it, Maudie and me,
Because it's the All Alone, All Alone Tree.

In the bright summer-time when they're cutting
    the hay,
Then the birds come and sing in its branches all
    day
And we're awfully glad of this Maudie and me,
Because it's the All Alone, All Alone Tree.

But in the dark winter the birds have all flown,
And we know that it's standing there, quite, quite
    alone,
So we creep out and kiss it then, Maudie and me,
Because it's the All Alone, All Alone Tree.

"Trees are much like human beings and enjoy each
other's company. Only a few love to be alone."
John Muir

## THE LEGEND OF ST. NICHOLAS

Helen Hunt Jackson (1830-1885), published in *Bits of Talk, in Verse and Prose, for Young Folks*, 1892

... Hurrah for good St. Nicholas!
The friend of all the poor,
Who never sent a little child
Unsuccored* from his door.

We do not pray to saints today,
But still we hold them dear,
And the stories of their holy lives
Are stories good to hear.

They are a sort of parable,
And if we ponder well,
We shall not find it hard to read
The lesson which they tell.

We do not pray to saints today,
Yet who knows but they hear
Our mention of them, and are glad
We hold their memory dear?

Hurrah for good St. Nicholas,
The friend of all the poor,
Who never sent a little child
Unsuccored from his door.

\* Unaided; with no help

"So then you are no longer strangers and sojourners, but you are fellow citizens with the holy ones and members of the household of God, built upon the foundation of the apostles and prophets with Christ Jesus himself as the capstone." – Ephesians 2:19-20

## THE FIRST SNOWFALL (FROM)
James Russell Lowell (1819-1891), published in
*Heath Readers: Fourth Reader,* 1903

T he snow had begun in the gloaming,
   And busily all the night
Had been heaping field and highway
   With a silence deep and white.
Every pine and fir and hemlock
   Wore ermine too dear for an earl,
And the poorest twig on the elm tree
   Was ridged inch deep with pearl. . . .
I stood and watched by the window
   The noiseless work of the sky,
And the sudden flurries of snow-birds,
   Like brown leaves whirling by.
Up spoke our own little Mabel,
   Saying, "Father, who makes it snow?"
And I told of the good All-father
   Who cares for us here below. . . .

"Silence is the great unknown power source, the
great untapped resource. Silence is more than noise,
not less." – Peter Kreeft

## TO MARY IMMACULATE

Sister Maryanna, O.P., published in
*A Lovely Gate Set Wide*, 1946

Patroness of our loved land,
  Maiden Mother pure,
Guard thine own America
  From all harm secure.
Radiant with sanctity,
  Be thyself our light.
Guide our nation's destinies,
  Thou wilt lead aright.
By thy mystic crown of stars,
  By thy mantle's hue,
Keep our starry banner high,
  Help us to be true.
Let thy smile rest tenderly
  On our country's youth.
School their hearts in honor, faith,
  Purity, and truth.
Thou by God's foreshadowing
  Kept from sin-stain free,
Pray for us who have recourse,
  Virgin, fair, to thee!

"A great sign appeared in the sky, a woman clothed
with the sun, with the moon under her feet, and on
her head a crown of twelve stars." – Revelation 12:1

## JACK FROST
Published in *Songs of the*
*Tree-top and Meadow*, 1899

Jack Frost comes round here every year

He's such a shy old elf,
Whate'er he sees he wants to bite,—
He's sure to help himself.
O, Jack Frost, it troubles us to see
How very, very impolite
A boy like you can be.
Sometimes he's stinging at your ears,
And then he's at your toes.
Whene'er you chase him off of these
He's nipping at your nose.

"Frost and chill, bless the Lord;
praise and exalt him above all forever."
Daniel 3:69

## WINTER'S BLESSINGS

William Allen Bixler (1876-1961), published in
*Light on the Child's Path*, 1918

Pretty little snowflakes
Falling to the ground;
Here is one, there is one,
Everywhere they're found.

See them fall so gently
Through the frosty air;
Every little snowflake
Has its beauties rare.

Soon the ground is covered
With the pretty snow;
Then we see the snowbirds
Flying to and fro.

Happy little creatures—
Do not reap or sow;
Yet the Master feeds them,
Even in the snow. . . .

"If you truly love nature, you will find beauty
everywhere." – Vincent van Gogh

## I HEARD A BIRD SING

Oliver Herford (1863-1935), published in
*Association Monthly, Volume 8,* 1915

I heard a bird sing
In the dark of December.
A magical thing
And sweet to remember.

"We are nearer to Spring
Than we were in September,"
I heard a bird sing
In the dark of December.

"A bird does not sing because it has an answer; it sings
because it has a song." – Maya Angelou

December 12
Our Lady of Guadalupe

## Song to the Virgin Mary

Pero Lopez de Ayala (1332-1407), published in
*Hispanic Anthology*, 1920

Lady, as I know thy power,

I place my hopes in thee;
Thy shrine in Guadalupe's tower
My pilgrim steps shall see. . . .

In all my sorrows would I call
On thee, Sweet Advocate;
My heart adores thee more than all,
And so my sins seem great.

Thou art the star that shows the way,
The balm that heals my wrong;
In gentleness be mine today
And lead to heaven along.

Lady, as I know thy power,
I place my hopes in thee;
Thy shrine in Guadalupe's tower
My pilgrim steps shall see.

"Rejoice in hope, endure in affliction, persevere in
prayer." – Romans 12:12

## THE MAN IN THE MOON
Traditional Rhyme

The Man in the Moon as he sails the sky
Is a very remarkable skipper,
But he made a mistake when he tried to take
A drink of milk from the Dipper.
He dipped right out of the Milky Way,
And slowly and carefully filled it,
The Big Bear growled, and the Little Bear howled
And frightened him so that he spilled it!

## THE PRESENT
Mary Carolyn Davies (1888-1940?), published in
*A Little Freckled Person*, 1919

The sky is like a Christmas tree,
The burning stars its candles be;
The moon's a bulky gift and odd,
Marked, "To the World, With Love,
From God."

"I would gaze upon the *stars* which were twinkling
ever so peacefully in the skies and the sight carried
me away." – St. Therese of Lisieux

## 'FRAID STARS

Mary Carolyn Davies (1888-1940?), published in
*A Little Freckled Person*, 1919

The stars are like us children here,

Not any older grown;
At night, the little 'fraid stars stay
Together in the Milky Way—
The brave ones stand alone!

## STAR-CASTE

Mary Carolyn Davies (1888-1940?), published in
*A Little Freckled Person*, 1919

A star looked down upon the sea,

And to a lighthouse trim said he,
"I wonder what you are!"
The lighthouse twinkled instantly,
"Why, you're the aristocracy,
And I'm a working star!"

"The best remedy for those who are afraid, lonely, or
unhappy is to go outside, somewhere where they can
be quiet, alone with the heavens, nature and God,
because only then does one feel that all is
as it should be." – Anne Frank

## JOSEPH'S THOUGHTS
Rev. Edward F. Garesche (1876-1960), published in
*The Four Gates*, 1913

Jesus' words and Mary's
Oft the Gospels tell.
Glad we read them over,
Pondering them well.
Sweetnesses of heaven
In the pages dwell.

Then we gently wonder:
"All the pages through
Never word from Joseph?"
Hark, the answer due:
Jesus' thoughts, and Mary's,
They were Joseph's, too.

"So, if you are too tired to speak, sit next to me,
because I too am fluent in silence." – R. Arnold

## THE CHRISTMAS TREE
Mary A. McHugh, published in
*Child's Calendar Beautiful,* 1905

Y ou come from a land where the snow lies deep
In forest glade, on mountain steep,
Where the days are short and the nights are long.
And never a skylark sings his song.
Have you seen the wild deer in his mountain home,
And watched the fall of the brown pine cone?
Do you miss your mates in the land of snow,
Where none but the evergreen branches grow?
Dear tree, we will dress you in robes so bright
That ne'er could be seen a prettier sight;
In glittering balls and tinkling bells.
And the star which the story of Christmas tells;
On every branch we will place a light
That shall send its gleam through the starry night;
And the little children will gather there,
And carol their songs in voices fair;
And we hope you will never homesick be,
You beautiful, beautiful Christmas tree.

"And so it is whenever we go into the woods: There is
always the searching, and one never knows what one
may find." – Sigurd Olson

## THE CHERUB FOLK
Enid Dinnis (1873-1942), published in
*Meadowsweet and Thyme*, 1922

In highest heaven, at Mary's knee,
The Cherubs sit with folded wings,
And beg her by St. Charity
To tell them tales of human things.

They throw their harps down on the floor,
And all their heavenly playthings leave,
And clamor to be told once more
The faerie tale of faulty Eve.

Up into Mary's lap they climb
To hear how on a place called Earth
Once, in a wondrous thing called Time
The Uncreated One had birth.

And she to whom a Son was given,
Plays there her mother's part to them
And tells the Cherub folk in heaven
The wonder tale of Bethlehem.

"Although the angels are superior to us in many ways,
yet in some respects . . . they fall short of us with
regard to being in the image of the Creator; for we,
rather than they, have been created in God's image."
St. Gregory Palamas

## WHY I AM HAPPY AT CHRISTMAS

Sister Mary Josita Belger (1899-1978), published in
*Sing a Song of Holy Things*, 1945

Fairy snowflakes fell today
    Upon each house and tree.
They made me very happy
    Because I knew, you see,

That Christmas comes when snowflakes fall
    And when the wind is cold.
Oh, I know all about it
    Without having to be told.

I suppose you think I'm happiest
    Because Santa Claus will come
When Jack Frost nips our noses
    And make our fingers numb.

It's true I like to see him
    With his reindeer and his toys;
But that's not the only reason,
    Nor the best for girls and boys.

It's because the Baby Jesus
    Comes to us on Christmas Day.
Even though He made the heavens,
    You will find Him in the hay.

But this Christmas I'll surprise Him
    With my heart a cradle-bed,
With a soft and downy pillow
    For His little curly head.

"At Christmas I no more desire a rose,
Than wish a snow in May's new-fangled mirth."
William Shakespeare

## THE FOREST SCHOOL
Mary Carolyn Davies (1888-1940?), published in
*A Little Freckled Person*, 1919

The little firs demurely stand
In studious rows, on either hand,
On winter days about like these,
All learning to be Christmas trees.

"I never found a companion that was so
companionable as solitude." – Henry David Thoreau

## THE CHRIST CANDLE

Kate Louise Brown (1837-1921), published in
*The Journal of Education, Volume 87*, 1918

Little taper set tonight,
Throw afar thy tiny light;
Up and down the darksome street,
Guide the tender, loving feet
Of the darling Christ Child sweet.

He is coming in the snow
As he came so long ago.
When the star set o'er the hill
When the town is dark and still,
Comes to do the Father's will.

Little taper spread thy way,
Make his pathway light as day;
Let some door be opened wide
For this guest of Christmastide,
Dearer than all else beside.

Little Christ Child, come to me,
Let my heart thy shelter be;
Such a home thou wilt not scorn,
So, the bells of Christmas morn
Glad shall sing "A Christ is born!"

"I try always to be a Bethany for Jesus, so that He may
rest here after all His labor." – St. Faustina Kowalska,
*Divine Mercy in My Soul*, 735

## I'M WISHING THE WHOLE WORLD CHRISTMAS
Annette Wynne (died 1953), published in
*For Days and* Days, 1919

I'm wishing the whole world Christmas—
  The children, the beasts, and the birds;
I'm wishing the whole world Christmas—
  And I'd like to have magical words
To wish just the shining wish I would wish
  In the Christmas words I would say,
For I'm wishing the whole world Christmas,
  And joy on Christmas Day.

O, I'd need a pen to write golden,
  The goldenest pen indeed,
To wish the whole world Christmas
  For the happy children to read.
I'm wishing the whole world Christmas
  And may the dear Lord be kind,
And send blessings down like snowflakes
  For all of His children to find . . .

"The LORD bless you and keep you!
The LORD let his face shine upon you, and be
gracious to you!
The LORD look upon you kindly and give you peace!"
Numbers 6:24-26

## CAROL FOR SLEEPY CHILDREN
Sister Maris Stella (1916-2013), published in
*Here Only a Dove*, 1939

When Mary came to Bethlehem
On the first Christmas night,
She bore the lovely Christ-Child
To be each child's delight.

There was no room in Bethlehem
For anyone so small
And yet so great as Mary's Child
But in an ox's stall.

There was no bed in Bethlehem
For anyone so poor
And yet so rich as Mary's Child
But on the stable floor.

Oh, all you little children
Who sleep in linen white,
Would you not share your cradles,
If Jesus came tonight?

"'And this will be a sign for you: you will find an infant wrapped in swaddling clothes and lying in a manger.'" – Luke 2:12

## CHRISTMAS WISH

Sister Mary Josita Belger (1899-1978), published in
*Sing a Song of Holy Things*, 1945

I wish I could have been on earth

When Mary came to Bethlehem,
And Joseph went from house to house
To find a sheltering home for them.

I would have asked my mom and dad
To give them shelter from the cold.
And when the Baby Jesus came,
What happiness 'twould be to hold

My little Lord the live-long day,
And tell Him stories of the stars,
And show Him pretty picture-books
With trees and animals and flowers.

And oh, how happy He would be
To know I like the things He made,
For that same little Baby boy
Would be the God to Whom I prayed.

And when the Baby grew a bit
We'd walk out in the summer air,
And all my friends would be surprised
To see this lovely Child play there.

If I had only been on earth
That time so many years ago
I would have opened wide my door
To shelter Jesus from the snow.

"Ever since the creation of the world, his invisible
attributes of eternal power and divinity have been
able to be understood and perceived in what he has
made." – Romans 1:20

## CHRISTMAS EVERYWHERE

Phillip Brooks (1835-1893), published in
*Christmas Songs and Easter Carols*, 1903

Everywhere, everywhere, Christmas tonight!
Christmas in lands of the fir-tree and pine,
Christmas in lands of the palm-tree and vine,
Christmas where snow peaks stand solemn
    and white,
Christmas where cornfields stand sunny and
    bright.
Everywhere, everywhere, Christmas tonight!

Christmas where children are hopeful and gay,
Christmas where old men are patient and gray,
Christmas where peace, like a dove in his flight,
Broods o'er brave men in the thick of the fight;
Everywhere, everywhere, Christmas tonight!

For the Christ-child who comes is the Master
    of all;
No palace too great, no cottage too small.

"'Glory to God in the highest
and on earth peace to those on whom his favor
rests.'" – Luke 2:14

## BABY JESUS

Caro A. Dugan, published in "The Kindergarten
Magazine: Volume 9", 1896

Oh, it was in the noon of night,
The heavens with stars were crowded bright,
And one star showed, with wondrous light,
Baby Jesus.

Sweet Mary Mother knelt to pray,
Beside the simple bed of hay,
Within a manger rude, where lay
Baby Jesus.

The shining angels through the sky
Sang "Glory be to God most high,
And peace on earth, for there doth lie
Baby Jesus."

The wond'ring cattle stood around;
The wise men knelt upon the ground;
The Savior of the world is found—
Baby Jesus.

"A God who became so small could only be mercy
and love." – St. Therese of Lisieux

## FEAST O' SAINT STEPHEN
### (FROM "THE VOYAGE OF THE WEE RED CAP")
Ruth Sawyer (1880-1970), published in "The Outlook"
weekly newspaper, 1911

Listen all ye, 'tis the Feast o' Saint Stephen,
Mind that ye keep it, this holy even.
Open your door and greet ye the stranger,
For ye mind that the wee Lord had naught but
manger.

Feed ye the hungry and rest ye the weary,
This ye must do for the sake of Our Mary.
'Tis well that ye mind—ye who sit by the fire—
That the Lord He was born in a dark and cold byre.*

\* a cowshed

## GOOD NIGHT
Fr. John Tabb (1845-1909),
published in *A Selection from the Verses
of John B. Tabb*, 1907

Good night, dear Lord! and now,
Let them that loved to keep
Your little bed in Bethlehem
Be near me while I sleep. . . .

"We tend to demean contemplative rest as
something unproductive and unnecessary, but this is
to do away with the very thing which is most
important about work: its meaning." – *Laudato Si'* 237

December 27

## GOOD NIGHT, DEAR BABY JESUS
Sister Mary Josita Belger  (1899-1978), published in
*Sing a Song of Holy Things*, 1945

Good night, dear Baby Jesus!
The church is dark and still,
That's why I came away from play,
And ran along until
I saw Your home with golden cross
Pointing to the sky.
And here I am my little Lord.
I'll go back by and by.
The vigil lights are twinkling,
Green and gold and red.
They move in lovely shadows
Around your curly head.
And oh, the Christmas trees smell sweet.
They stand so tall and grand,
They make me think of story-books
And things in fairyland.
I hope You won't be lonely
Here in the dark, dark night.
Angels will watch over You
Until the day comes bright.
I'll leave you now, sweet Baby,
In Mother Mary's care.
Her tender arms will hug You tight,
Her heart Your sorrows share. . . .
I'll be right her to talk to you
As soon as it is light.
Then go to sleep, dear little Lord,
Good night, little Love, good night!

"What we need most in order to make progress is to be silent before this great God with our appetites and our tongue, for the language He best hears is silent love." – St. John of the Cross

## FOR DECEMBER 28

Mary Fabyan Windeatt (1910-1979), published in
*Sing Joyfully*, 1942

The little Holy Innocents
Who perished by the sword
Two thousand years have gone about
The gardens of the Lord;
And though by now they should be old,
With long grey beards, or white,
The little Holy Innocents
Are two years old tonight.

In Bethlehem of Palestine
Their dreadful death was done,
But God has blessed their severed throats
And given them the sun,
The moon and stars to realize,
His saints to love and know—
Those little boys of Bethlehem
Who died so long ago. . . .

Tonight the Holy Innocents
Are merry in their song.
They know their Alleluia well
For they have practiced long.
*"A Child is born, a Son is given!"*
And so is Christmas sung
By heaven's Christmas martyrlings—
So old, and yet so young!

"To love you here on earth, Jesus, I only have today."
St. Therese of Lisieux

## ST. THOMAS BECKET OF CANTERBURY

Robert Hugh Benson (1871-1914), published in
*An Alphabet of Saints*, 1906

**"T"** is also a Martyr, ST. THOMAS I mean,
The bravest Archbishop that ever was seen.
St. THOMAS was Primate of England, and fought
For the rights of the Church which the King set at
    nought;
So they quarreled, these two, for a very long time,
Until Henry the Second committed this crime:—
He threatened St. THOMAS'S death, or at least
He said, "Who will *get rid* of this pestilent Priest?"
Fitz Urse and De Morville and Richard Le Breton
And William De Tracey, who heard the King
    threaten,
Rode off to the Abbey of CHRIST Church in Kent
And slew the good Priest the King called "pestilent,"
On the last day but two in the month of December—
A date which all Englishmen used to remember,
Till Harry the Eighth, who had made himself Pope,*
Broke St. THOMAS'S statues in Mitre and Cope;
Yet still, where at Lambeth his empty niche stands,
Thames bargemen salute him with reverent hands.

* "He would be the King, the whole King, and nothing but
the King; he would be the Pope, the whole Pope, and
something more than the Pope."—Stubbs.

(St. Thomas Of Canterbury, Bishop and Martyr; Born in
London, December 21, 1118; Consecrated Archbishop of
Canterbury, 1152; Martyred, 1166. Feast, December 29)

"All saints give testimony to the truth that without real
effort, no one ever wins the crown."
St. Thomas Becket

## BETHLEHEM OF JUDEA
Published in *Poetry Time*, 1953

A little child,
A shining star,
A stable rude,
The door ajar,

Yet in this place,
So rude, forlorn,
The Hope of all
The world was born.

## SON OF GOD
Charles L. O'Donnell, published in
*Dreams and Images* by Joyce Kilmer, 1917

The fount of Mary's joy
Revealed now lies,
For, lo, has not the Boy
His Father's eyes?

"The Son of God became a man to enable men to become sons of God." – C. S. Lewis, *Mere Christianity*

## A SERENADE FOR NEW YEAR'S EVE

Francis J. Crosby (1820-1915), published in *Documents of the Senate of the State of New York: Volume 1*, 1845

The old year departed, how swiftly it flew,
'Tis gone, and with rapture we welcome the new;—
We trust a bright morning will dawn on your eyes,—
And sun beams unclouded illumine the skies.
Then wake from your slumbers, our serenade hear,—
We wish you a happy, a happy New Year!

"Be at war with your vices, at peace with your neighbors, and let every new year find you a better man." — Benjamin Franklin

# JANUARY

## JANUARY
Alice E. Allen, published in
*Primary Education: Volume 9*, 1901

Sparkling world and shining sky,
Sleigh-bells jingling, jangling by,
Skates that gleam and sleds that fly,
Make up January.

Snowy world and low hung cloud,
Snowflakes whirling in a crowd,
Winds a-whistling long and loud.
Make up January.

Snow and shine and shine and snow.
Days that swiftly come and go,
Thirty-one of them, you know,
Make up January.

"RISING VERY EARLY BEFORE DAWN, HE LEFT AND WENT OFF TO A DESERTED PLACE, WHERE HE PRAYED." – MARK 1:35

## THE WELCOME

Leonard Feeney (1897-1978), published in
*In Towns and Little Towns*, 1927

No music He heard, and no angels He saw
As He lay in His wrappings of linen and straw;
And the ox and the ass could not kneel and adore
For the poor creatures never were angels before.

The palace He found was an old cattle stall
With a broken-down roof and a windowless wall,
And it looked so ashamed of its spider-worn wood;
But it tried to be Heaven, as well as it could.

A dull stable-lantern that hung dark and dim
Was the small bit of moonlight that flickered on
   Him.
Now it longed to be beautiful, starry and bright;
And it sputtered and wept for the dearth of its light.

But a Lady of Beauty stood over His head
While she gathered the strewings about for His bed.
And her soul was as sweet as a fresh-budding rose
And as white as the fusion of myriad snows.

And her hands did not soil this immaculate prize,
And her breath did not sully the bloom in His eyes.
On her breast sweet and safe could He slumber
   and nod:
The lily-white village-maid, Mother of God.

"Once in our world, a stable had something in it that
was bigger than our whole world." – C.S. Lewis

## THE NEW YEAR
Dinah M. Craik (1826-1887), published in
*Brooke's Readers: Volume 4*, 1906

Who comes dancing over the snow,
His soft little feet all bare and rosy?
Open the door, though the wild wind blow,
Take the child in and make him cozy,
Take him in and hold him dear,
Here is the wonderful glad New Year.

## A THOUGHT FOR THE NEW YEAR
Published in
*Among Ourselves: Volume 4*, 1907

Just to be tender, just to be true;
Just to be glad the whole day through;
Just to be merciful, just to be mild;
Just to be trustful as a child;
Just to be gentle and kind and sweet;
Just to be helpful with willing feet;
Just to be cheery when things go wrong;
Just to drive sadness away with a song;
Whether the hour is dark or bright;
Just to be loyal to God and right;
Just to believe that God knows best;
Just in His promise ever to rest;
Just to let love be our daily key;
This is God's will, for you and me.

"Resolution One: I will live for God. Resolution Two: If
no one else does, I still will." – Jonathan Edwards

## THE HOLY NAME OF JESUS

Sister Mary Josita Belger (1899-1978), published in
*Sing a Song of Holy Things*, 1945

O h, blessed Name of Jesus!
Name of God's dear Son!
I bow my head and bend my knee
On hearing it begun.

Oh, tender Name of Jesus!
Sweetest ever heard!
I hope that on my dying lips
Will be that blessed word.

Oh, holy Name of Jesus!
Joy of angel bands!
Blest forever be that Name
In this and all the lands.

"that at the name of Jesus
every knee should bend,
of those in heaven and on earth and under the earth,
and every tongue confess that
Jesus Christ is Lord,
to the glory of God the Father." – Philippians 2:10-11

## SWEETEST BABY JESUS
Cecil Hope, published in *Seabury Castle*, 1869

Child:

O sweetest Baby Jesus,
In the manger poor and low,
What can I do to warm You
From the winter's cold and snow?

Infant Jesus:
Dear little child so thoughtful,
I am far from my home above,
So build a crib within your heart,
And warm Me with your love.

"What lies behind us and what lies before us are
tiny matters compared to what lies within us. And
when you bring what is within out into the world,
miracles happen." – Ralph Waldo Emerson

# THE SHEPHERD BOY

Sister Mary Josita Belger (1899-1978), published
*Sing a Song of Holy Things*, 1945

When I kneel down before the crib
With lights all twinkling round,
I wish I were the shepherd boy
Who knelt there on the ground,
With woolly lambs in both his arms,
Wee little lambs of white,
Bleating with a tender cry
And trembling in the night.

The little shepherd boy who had
No gift of shining gold,
But when he saw the little Lord
Lie shivering in the cold,
He asked his shepherd father,
"Please, Father, may I bring
This little Babe my two pet lambs?
I have no other thing."

The father answered with a nod,
And smiled upon his son.
The woolly little lambs were then
Brought to the Holy One.
While Mary and Saint Joseph
Looked upon the shepherd boy,
The Baby Jesus blessed him,
And filled his heart with joy.

"When the angels went away from them to heaven,
the shepherds said to one another, 'Let us go, then, to
Bethlehem to see this thing that has taken place,
which the Lord has made known to us.' So they went
in haste and found Mary and Joseph, and the infant
lying in the manger." – Luke 2:15-16

## A CHILD'S OFFERING
Edward J. Hopkins (1818-1901), published in
*Book of Praise for Children*, 1881

The wise may bring their learning,

The rich may bring their wealth,
And some may bring their greatness,
And some their strength and health.

We too would bring our treasures
To offer to the King.
We have no wealth or learning—
What treasures shall we bring?

We'll bring hearts filled with loving,
We'll bring our thankful praise,
While always humbly trying
To follow in God's ways.

## THE SANCTUARY LAMP
Yvonne Dolphin, published in
*Religious Poems for Little Folks*, 1936

A little star
Did Magi bring
In land afar
To Christ the King.

A ruby light
In chapel dim
Bids all tonight
To come to Him.

"and on entering the house they saw the child with
Mary his mother. They prostrated themselves and did
him homage. Then they opened their treasures and
offered him gifts of gold, frankincense, and myrrh."
Matthew 2:11

## THE GARDEN YEAR
Sara Coleridge (1802-1852), published in
*Poems of Youth and Age*, 1915

January brings the snow,
Makes our feet and fingers glow.
February brings the rain,
Thaws the frozen lake again.
March brings breezes, loud and shrill,
To stir the dancing daffodil.
April brings the primrose sweet,
Scatters daisies at our feet.
May brings flocks of pretty lambs
Skipping by their fleecy dams.
June brings tulips, lilies, roses,
Fills the children's hands with posies.
Hot July brings cooling showers,
Apricots, and gillyflowers.
August brings the sheaves of corn,
Then the harvest home is borne.
Warm September brings the fruit;
Sportsmen then begin to shoot.
Fresh October brings the pheasant;
Then to gather nuts is pleasant.
Dull November brings the blast;
Then the leaves are whirling fast.
Chill December brings the sleet,
Blazing fire, and Christmas treat.

"Sunshine is delicious, rain is refreshing, wind braces us
up, snow is exhilarating; there is no such thing as bad
weather just different kinds of good weather."
John Ruskin

## THREE CHEERS FOR OLD WINTER
Frank H. Sweet (1865-1919), published in
*School Education: Volumes 28-29*, 1909

Three cheers for Old Winter, so royal and grand,
    With his robe of glistening white.
We hail him with joy, as the King of the Year,
    He brings us such perfect delight.
What sports are so fine as come in his train,
    What snow-balling, sledding, and fun;
What riotous games we are reveling in,
    What glorious races we run. . . .

Three cheers for Old Winter, so royal and grand,
    With his wonderful keys; he is here;
With one, he has sealed and fastened secure
    The dead and departed Old Year.
He let out the Old and let in the New,
    This honor's entirely his own.
No other season, at least in these parts,
    So grand a distinction has known.

"The world is charged with the grandeur of God."
Gerard Manley Hopkins

## FALLING SNOW
Published in
*Poetry for the Young: A Collection,* 1881

See the pretty snowflakes
Falling from the sky;
On the wall and housetops
Soft and thick they lie.

On the window ledges,
On the branches bare;
Now how fast they gather,
Filling all the air.

Look into the garden,
Where the grass was green;
Covered by the snowflakes,
Not a blade is seen.

Now the bare black bushes
All look soft and white,
Every twig is laden,—
What a pretty sight!

"The lovely stormy wings of snow." – A. C. Swinburne

## WINTER DAYS

Daniel A. Lord (1888-1955), published in
*Chants for Children*, 1942

Who says it's chill?
Who says it's cold?
Down, temperature!
Up, spirits bold!
For skates come out
And sleds appear,
And snowballs fly,
And children cheer.
And Santa rides
His magic sleigh,
And parties fill
The winter day.
And appetites
Are sharp and keen,
And rooms are bright
With evergreen.
And boys and girls
Galoshing go
To slide and tumble
In the snow.
With skates and skis
And sleds and sleighs,
We thanks the Lord
For winter days.

"Cold and chill, bless the Lord;
praise and exalt him above all forever. . . .
Hoarfrost and snow, bless the Lord;
praise and exalt him above all forever."
Daniel 3:67, 70

January 11

## SNOWFLAKES (FROM)
Henry Wadsworth Longfellow (1807-1882), published in
*The Poetical Works of Henry Wadsworth Longfellow,*
1886

. . . Over the woodlands brown and bare,
Over the harvest-fields forsaken
Silent, and soft, and slow
Descends the snow. . . .

## SNOW SONG
Sara Teasdale (1884-1933), published in
*Helen of Troy and Other Poems,* 1911

Fairy snow, fairy snow,
Blowing, blowing everywhere,
Would that I
Too, could fly
Lightly, lightly through the air.

"We need to find God, and he cannot be found in
noise and restlessness. God is the friend of silence. See
how nature—trees, flowers, grass—grows in silence;
see the stars, the moon and the sun, how they move
in silence. . . . We need silence to be able to touch
souls." – St. Teresa of Calcutta

## THE SEASONS
Helen Adelaide Richer, published in *Nature in Verse,*
*A Poetry Reader for Children*, 1895

Our babies lay in their cradles new,
Beginning to think of "What shall I do
The world to brighten and beautify?"
The Spring baby first said, "Let me try."

So she put on a dress of freshest green,
With trimmings the loveliest ever seen—
Trimmings of tulips and hyacinths rare
And trailing arbutus looped everywhere.

"How perfectly beautiful!" Summer said;
"But wait till you see my dress of red
And darker green with golden spots,
Trimmed with roses and pinks and forget-me-nots."

"Pooh!" said Autumn, "My dress will be
A more substantial one, you'll see;
With skirt of finest and yellowest wheat,
A girdle of grapes and squash turban neat."

Then Winter came silently tripping along.
Chanting softly a Christmas song.
In a pure white dress with jewels spread,
Holding a basket of books on his head,

Poems and stories and pictures were there
Of the Christ child, the Yule log of folk-lore rare.
"I am not in bright colors," he said, with a smile,
"But the long winter evenings my gifts here beguile."

"In the winter she curls up around a good book and
dreams away the cold." – Ben Aaronovitch

## WERE I THE SUN
Amos R. Wells (1862-1933), published in
*Primary Education: Volume 4*, 1896

I'd always shine on holidays
    Were I the sun;
On sleepy heads I'd never gaze,
But focus all my morning rays
On busy folks of hustling ways,
    Were I the sun.

I would not melt a sledding snow,
    Were I the sun;
Nor spoil the ice where skaters go,
Nor help those useless weeds to grow,
But hurry melons on you know,
    Were I the sun.

I'd warm the swimming pool just right,
    Were I the sun;
On school-days I would hide my light.
The Fourth I'd always give you bright,
Nor set so soon on Christmas night,
    Were I the sun.

I would not heed such paltry* toys,
    Were I the sun—
Such work as grown-up men employs;
But I would favor solid joys—
In short I'd run the world for boys,
    Were I the sun!

\* small; unimportant

> "'You are the light of the world. . . . your light must
> shine before others, that they may see your good
> deeds and glorify your heavenly Father.'"
> Matthew 5:14, 16

## THE SNOWFALL
Published in *The Winter Months*, 1907

Old Winter comes forth in his robe of white;
He sends the sweet flowers far out of sight;
He robs the trees of their green leaves quite,
　　And freezes the pond and the river.

He has spoiled the butterfly's pretty vest,
And ordered the birds not to build their nest.
And banished the frog to a four months' rest.
　　And makes all the children shiver.

Yet he does some good with his icy tread,
For he keeps the corn seeds warm in their bed,
He dries up the damp which the rain had spread,
　　And renders the air more healthy.

We like the spring with its fine fresh air;
We like the summer with flowers so fair;
We like the fruits we in autumn share.
　　And we like, too, old winter's greeting.

"I go to nature to be soothed and healed, and to
have my senses put in order." – John Burroughs

## CHICKADEE
Ralph Waldo Emerson (1803-1882), published in
"Birds and Nature" magazine, 1905

Then piped a tiny voice hard by,

Gay and polite, a cheerful cry,
"Chick-a-dee-dee!" a saucy note
Out of sound heart and merry throat
As if it said, "Good day, good sir!
Fine afternoon, old passenger!
Happy to meet you in these places
Where January brings few faces."

## THE CHICKADEE
May Morgan, published in *140 Folk Songs with Piano
Accompaniment*, 1922

Trees are bare everywhere,

Snows are deep and skies are gray;
Yet one bird may be heard on the coldest day.
Ask his name and he'll reply,
Cocking up a roguish eye,
"Chick-a-dee, Chick-a-dee, Chick-a-dee-dee-dee."

Jolly chap with a cap
Soft as velvet, black as night,
He's so gay, Quaker gray,
Does not suit him quite.
Most unlike his sober coat
Is his bright and cheery note,
"Chick-a dee, Chick-a-dee, Chick-a-dee-dee-dee."

"But above all of them ranked the chickadee
because of its indomitable spirit."
Tom Brown, Jr., *The Tracker*

## SING, LITTLE BIRD
Published in *American Primary Teacher*, 1910

Sing, little bird, when the skies are blue,
Sing, for the world has need of you,
Sing when the skies are overcast,
Sing when the rain is falling fast.

Sing, happy heart, when the sun is warm,
Sing in the winter's coldest storm,
Sing little songs, O heart so true,
Sing, for the world has need of you.

"In order to see birds it is necessary to become part of the silence." – Robert Lynd

## WHITE FIELDS

James Stephens (1882-1950), published in
*The Rocky Road to Dublin*, 1915


In the winter time we go

Walking in the fields of snow;
Where there is no grass at all;
Where the top of every wall,
Every fence and every tree,
Is as white, as white can be.

Pointing out the way we came,
Everyone of them the same—
All across the fields there be
Prints in silver filigree*;
And our mothers always know,
By our footprints in the snow,
Where it is the children go.


*lacework; ornamental wire decoration

"In every walk with nature, one receives far more
than he seeks." – John Muir

## WINTER NIGHT

Mary F. Butts (1890-1937), published in *The Posy Ring:
A Book of Verse for Children,* 1908

Blow, wind, blow!
Drift the flying snow!
Send it twirling, whirling overhead!
There's a bedroom in a tree,
Where, snug as snug can be,
The squirrel nests in his cozy bed.

Shriek, wind, shriek!
Make the branches creak!
Battle with the boughs till break o' day!
In a snow-cave warm and tight,
Through the icy winter night
The rabbit sleeps the peaceful hours away.

Call, wind, call,
In entry and in hall,
Straight from off the mountain white and wild!
Soft purrs the pussy cat,
On her little fluffy mat,
And beside her nestles close her furry child.

Scold, wind, scold,
So bitter and so bold!
Shake the windows with your tap, tap, tap!
With half-shut, dreamy eyes,
The drowsy baby lies
Cuddled closely in his mother's lap.

"One day's exposure to mountains is better than
cartloads of books." – John Muir

## WEATHER

Published in *The Amateur Photographer and Photography: Volume 51*, 1921

Whether the weather be fine
Or whether the weather be not,
Whether the weather be cold
Or whether the weather be hot,
We'll weather the weather
Whatever the weather,
Whether we like it or not.

## THE FOUR SEASONS

Lines on a French calendar, 1791

Spring: showery, flowery, bowery
Summer: hoppy, croppy, poppy
Autumn: wheezy, sneezy, freezy
Winter: slippy, drippy, nippy

"I seek acquaintance with nature, to know her moods and manners." – Henry David Thoreau

## ST. SEBASTIAN

Robert Hugh Benson (1871-1914), published in
*An Alphabet of Saints*, 1906

**"S"** for SEBASTIAN bound to a tree,
And riddled with arrows by Caesar's decree;
When they loosed him he fell, and they thought
    he was slain,
But he rose and appeared before Caesar again;
At length he was cruelly cudgeled to death,
Confessing his LORD with his very last breath.
    A soldier who strove for no earthy renown,
    Twice he fought a good fight, and GOD gave
        him a crown.

(ST. SEBASTIAN, Martyr, called "Lay Apostle"; Born at Narbonne, about 265; Went to Rome in 284; Martyred at Rome about 288. Feast, January 20)

"Every athlete exercises discipline in every way. They do it to win a perishable crown, but we an imperishable one." – 1 Corinthians 9:25

January 21
St. Agnes

## GOD'S LITTLE LAMB

Sister Mary Josita Belger (1899-1978), published in
*Sing a Song of Holy Things*, 1945

Beautiful Agnes,
Flower of love,
God's sweet and fair little girl!

Lamb of the Savior,
Tender and true,
Dear one with long golden curl!

Look down from heaven,
Sweet little saint.
Teach small children to love.

Help us to follow you.
Pray for us daily, too.
Till we are with you above.

"The next day he saw Jesus coming toward him and said, 'Behold, the Lamb of God, who takes away the sin of the world.'" – John 1:29

## THE SNOW MAN
W. W. Ellsworth, published in
*Live Language Lessons: First Book*, 1917

One day we built a snow man;
  We made him out of snow.
You should have seen how fine he was—
  All white from top to toe!

We poured some water on him,
  And froze him, legs and ears;
And when we went indoors to bed
  I said he'd last two years.

But in the night a warmer kind
  Of wind began to blow,
And winter cried and ran away,
  And with it ran the snow.

And in the morning when we went
  To bid our friend good day,
There wasn't any snow man there—
  Everything had run away!

"Snowmen fall from heaven unassembled."
Unknown

## THE SQUIRREL

Alexina Black White (1830-1921), published in
*Little-Folk Songs*, 1880

Whisky, frisky,
Hippity hop;
Up he goes
To the tree top!

Whirly, twirly,
Round and round,
Down he scampers
To the ground.

Furly, curly
What a tail!
Tall as a feather
Broad as a sail!

Where's his supper?
In the shell,
Snappity, crackity,
Out it fell.

"The red squirrel is more common and less dignified
than the gray, and oftener guilty of petty larceny
about the barns and grain-fields." – John Burroughs

## THE SECRET
Published in *Poems for Memorization*, 1988

How does the busy squirrel know
The place where nuts and acorns grow?
What makes him pick them from the ground
And hide them where they can't be found?

How does he know on winter days
Just where his winter storehouse lays?
We know the secret, every whit;
God tells the squirrel all of it.

"Have you entered the storehouses of the snow,
and seen the storehouses of the hail . . . " – Job 38:22

## SNOW FLAKES

Mary Mapes Dodge (1831-1905), published in
*Along the Way*, 1879

Whenever a snowflake leaves the sky,

It turns and turns to say, "Good-bye!
Good-by, dear cloud, so cool and gray."
Then lightly travels on its way.

And when a snowflake finds a tree,
"Good-day," it says, "Good-day to thee."
Thou art so bare and lonely, dear,
I'll rest and call my comrades here."

But when a snowflake, brave and meek,
Lights on a maiden's rosy cheek.
It starts! "How warm and soft the day
'Tis summer!" And it melts away.

"It is the life of the crystal, the architect of the flake,
the fire of the frost, the soul of the sunbeam. This crisp
winter air is full of it." – John Burroughs

## CHECK

James Stephens (1882-1950), published in
*Collected Poems*, 1915

T he night was creeping on the ground;
She crept and did not make a sound
Until she reached the tree, and then
She covered it, and stole again
Along the grass beside the wall.

I heard the rustle of her shawl
As she threw blackness everywhere
Upon the sky and ground and air,
And in the room where I was hid:
But no matter what she did
To everything that was without,
She could not put my candle out.

So I stared at the night, and she
Stared back solemnly at me.

"Jesus spoke to them again, saying, 'I am the light of
the world. Whoever follows me will not walk in
darkness, but will have the light of life.'" – John 8:12

## THE SUN
### Amy Fiske, published in *The Spring Months*, 1907

I never go to sleep, dear child,
    I'm always shining bright,
But as your world goes turning round
    It takes you from my light.
And then I shine upon the moon
    And she shines back at you,
So that my light you often see
    When hidden from my view.

And as your world goes turning round
    It whirls you into night,
But brings round other boys and girls
    Into my shining light.
And so I shine, forever shine,
    While you both sleep and wake;
And now you've rolled around again
    My kind good morning take.

"I believe in Christianity as I believe that the sun has
risen: not only because I see it, but because by it I see
everything else." – C. S. Lewis

## A WINTER NIGHT

Sara Teasdale (1884-1933), published in
*Helen of Troy and Other Poems*, 1911

My window-pane is starred with frost,
The world is bitter cold tonight,
The moon is cruel and the wind
Is like a two-edged sword to smite.

God pity all the homeless ones,
The beggars pacing to and fro.
God pity all the poor tonight
Who walk the lamp-lit streets of snow.

"In rigorous hours, when down the iron lane
The redbreast looks in vain
For hips and haws,
Lo, shining flowers upon my window-pane
The silver pencil of the winter draws."
Robert Lewis Stevenson

## THE ICICLE

Mrs. Henry Gordon Gale, published in
*Songs of the Tree-top and Meadow*, 1899

$A$n icicle hung on a red brick wall,

And it said to the sun, "I don't like you at all!"
—Drip, drip, drip.

But the sun said, "Dear, you've a saucy tongue,
And you should remember, I'm old and you're
young."
—Drip, drip, drip.

But the icicle only cried the more,
Though the good sun smiled on it just as before,
Until at the end of the winter day,
It had cried its poor little self away!
—Drip - - drip - - - drip.

## ICICLES

Published in *The Instructor, Volume 57*, 1947

$W$e are little icicles
Melting in the sun.
Can you see our tiny teardrops
Falling one by one?

"Do not boast about tomorrow,
for you do not know what any day may bring forth."
Proverbs 27:1

## POLAR BEAR COAT
Published in *The Baby's Book of Baby Animals*, 2004

Polar bear,
Polar bear,
That's a wintry
Coat you wear.

Thick and warm,
It must be nice
For playing when
There's snow and ice.

While winter winds
Blow wild and free,
I'd like a coat like yours
For me!

## THE POLAR BEAR
Hilaire Belloc (1870-1953), published in
*The Bad Child's Book of Beasts*, 1896

The Polar Bear is unaware

Of cold that cuts me through:
For why? He has a coat of hair.
I wish I had one too!

"But now ask the beasts to teach you,
the birds of the air to tell you;
Or speak to the earth to instruct you,
and the fish of the sea to inform you.
Which of all these does not know
that the hand of God has done this?" - Job 12:7-9

## JANUARY COLD DESOLATE

Christina Rossetti (1830-1894), published in
*Sing Song, A Nursery Rhyme Book*, 1872

January cold desolate;
February all dripping wet;
March wind ranges;
April changes;
Birds sing in tune
To flowers of May,
And sunny June
Brings longest day;
In scorched July
The storm-clouds fly
Lightning-torn;
August bears corn,
September fruit;
In rough October
Earth must disrobe her;
Stars fall and shoot
In keen November;
And night is long
And cold is strong
In bleak December.

"So next is February,
So early in the spring:
The farmer ploughs the fallows,
The rooks their nests begin." – Old Rhyme

# FEBRUARY

## HERE IS FEBRUARY
Lettie Sterling, published in *Primary
Education: Volume 17*, 1907

Here is February—
Such a tiny thing;
She's the shortest daughter
Mother year can bring.

February sunbeams
Brighter grow each day,
Telling that the winter
Soon will pass away.

February sunshine
Melts the fallen snow;
And we see at noontime,
Little rivers flow.

February mornings
Frosty panes can show;
Still we're making snowballs;
Still the sleigh bells go.

Little February
Her little whims doth please;
If today she's thawing,
Soon she'll tightly freeze.

"Some people, to discover God, read books. But there is a great book: the very appearance of created things. Look above you! Look below you! Note it. Read it. God, whom you want to discover, never wrote that book with ink. Instead, He set before your eyes the things that He had made. Can you ask for a louder voice than that?" – St. Augustine

## THE SNOW BATTLE

Frank H. Sweet (1865-1919), published in
*School Education: Volumes 28-29*, 1909

From the signs of the times it is safe to say
That the big white fort will be stormed today;
The besiegers stand in battle array
 And the enemy takes position.
The drums are beaten, the trumpets blare,
And flags are fluttering everywhere,
And every resolute soldier there
 Has an armful of ammunition.

Their shout rings out in the frosty sky,
They pause—they charge—they waver and fly!
They halt—they form—and again they try,
 With reckless, wild endeavor.
Fiercer and closer the conflict grows,
Who cares now for a tingling nose?
He that first o'er the rampart goes
 Is covered with glory forever.

Thicker and faster the missiles fall.
Hark to the leader's stirring call;
"On! On! Over the wall!
 The enemy's ranks are shaken."
Bravely and blindly on they go
Facing a fearful volley of snow;
Now on the height their banners glow—
 Hurrah! for the fort is taken!

"Snowflakes are one of nature's most fragile things,
but just look what they can do when they stick
together." Vesta M. Kelly

## CANDLEMAS
Published in *The Virginia
Almanack for the Year 1765*

When New Year's Day is past and gone;
Christmas is with some people done;
But further some will it extend,
And at Twelfth Day their Christmas end:
Some people stretch it further yet,
At Candlemas they finish it.
The gentry carry it further still
And finish it just when they will;
They drink good wine, and eat good cheer,
And keep their Christmas all the year.

## THE FIRST DAY OF YULE (FROM)
Published in *Carols for Christmas*, 1861

. . . The fortieth day came Mary mild,
Into the temple with her child,
To show her clean that never was defiled,
And herewith endeth Christmas.

## CANDLEMAS DAY
Old English Poem (origin of Groundhog Day)

If Candlemas Day be fair and bright,
Winter will have another flight;
But if it be dark with clouds and rain,
Winter is gone, and will not come again.

Read "The Big Snow" picture book by Berta and Elmer
Hader for a story about Ground Hogs' Day.

## THE SNOW-BIRD
Frank Dempster Sherman (1860-1916), published in
*Nature Songs for Children,* 1906

When all the ground with snow is white,
The merry snow-bird comes,
And hops about with great delight
To find the scattered crumbs.

How glad he seems to get to eat
A piece of cake or bread!
He wears no shoes upon his feet,
Nor hat upon his head.

But happiest is he, I know,
Because no cage with bars
Keeps him from walking on the snow
And printing it with stars.

"There is no season such delight can bring
As summer, autumn, winter and the spring."
William Browne

## WINTER (FROM)
John Vance Cheney (1848-1922), published in
*The Rainbow Calendar*, 1888

So the brook in winter sings no more?
I grant he's gone in and shut the door;
But, bless you! He sings in much the same way
He sung as he ran down the meadows of May.
The brook (his old name, remember, was Elf)
Is cunning, keeping his tunes to himself.
I know very well he's not sung out;
And if you insist on good, full proof,
Just chip a hole in his palace roof.
Put down your ear, and make an end of doubt.

"The snow is melting into music."
John Muir

## FEBRUARY

Lucy Larcom (1824-1893), published in
*Our Little Tot's Speaker*, 1899

Month of spatters, splash and thaw,

Dreariest month I ever saw—
Dirty, wet and tiresome, very,—
February!

## THE SHORTEST MONTH

Adeline Whitney (1824-1906), published in
*Child's Calendar Beautiful*, 1906

Will Winter never be over?

Will the dark days never go?
Must the buttercup and clover
Be always hid under the snow?

Ah, lend me your little ear, love!
Hark! 'tis a beautiful thing;
The weariest month of the year, love,
Is shortest and nearest to spring.

"He who marvels at the beauty of the world in summer will find equal cause for wonder and admiration in winter." – John Burroughs

## SNOW
Mary Mapes Dodge (1831-1905), published in *Rhymes and Jingles*, 1874

Little white feathers, filling the air—
Little white feathers! How came you there?

"We came from the cloud-birds sailing so high;
They're shaking their white wings up in the sky."

Little white feathers, how swift you go!
Little white feathers, I love you so!

"We are swift because we have work to do;
But hold up your face, and we'll kiss you true."


## DIFFERENT WEATHER
J. M.L., published in *Weather Opinions*, 1907

Stormy little February
Muttered, "Horrid world this, very."
March rushed in all cross and weeping,
"Dirty world—needs lots of sweeping."
April murmured, "S'pose I try
To put sunshine in that sky."
May thought, as the leaves uncurled,
"What a very lovely world!"


"Always maintain a kind of summer even in the middle of winter." – Henry David Thoreau

## PUTTING THE WORLD TO BED

Esther W. Buxton, published in
*New Outlook: Volume 54*, 1896

The little Snow-people are hurrying down
From their home in the clouds overhead.
They are working as hard as ever they can,
Putting the world to bed.

Ev'ry tree in a soft fleecy nightgown they clothe;
Each part has its night-cap of white,
And o'er the cold ground a thick cover they spread
Before they say good-night.

And so they come eagerly sliding down
With a swift and silent tread,
Always as busy as busy can be,
Putting the world to bed.

"Kindness is like snow—it beautifies everything it
covers." – Kahlil Gibran

## MOTHER EARTH'S BEDQUILTS
S. Raymond Jocelyn, published in
*Our Little Tot's Speaker*, 1899

Four bedquilts are yearly folded and spread
On Mother Earth's old trundle-bed.
The first, a brown and white old thing,
She puts on in early spring.

The summer one is green and bright
With four-o'clocks, nodding left and right.
And then when winds begin to blow,
She spreads a red quilt on, you know.

She sews it through with yellow thread;
And makes an autumn-leaf bedspread.
And by and by, all in a night,
She spread her quilt of snowy white.

"I wonder if the snow loves the trees and fields, that it
kisses them so gently? And then it covers them up
snug, you know, with a white quilt; and perhaps it says
'Go to sleep, darlings, till the summer comes again.'"
Lewis Carroll, *Alice in Wonderland*

## O WIND

Christina Rossetti (1830-1894), published in
*Sing Song, A Nursery Rhyme Book*, 1872

O wind, why do you never rest

Wandering, whistling to and fro,
Bringing rain out of the west,
From the dim north bringing snow?

## AT NIGHT

Annie Willis McCullough (died 1916), published in
*In Playland*, 1911

The wind makes music all night long,

To lull a child to sleep—
Sometimes it sounds like mother's song
Sometimes an organ deep—
And overhead the stars stand still,
Like shining, watchful eyes.
How good God is, to always fill
The night with sweet surprise!

"The earth has music for those who listen."
William Shakespeare

## THE SNOW
Published in
*Songs of the Tree-top and Meadow*, 1899

From the clouds the flakes of snow
Wander to the world below,
    Falling lightly,
    Softly, whitely,
To the ground,
Heaping drifts without a sound.

Now the wind begins to blow,
Lighter, swifter, comes the snow,
    Falling thickly,
    Rushing quickly,
Soon there'll be
Castles built for you and me.

"He restores my soul." – Psalms 23:3

## THE NIGHT WORKMAN

Agnes S. Cook, published in *Primary Education:*
*Volume 4*, 1896

There is a fairy painter
   Who has lately been around,
But where he stays at daytime
   We children haven't found.

He comes when we are fast asleep
   And paints the window-pane.
With fairy trees and snow-white flowers,
   And then he comes again

And turns them into giants
   With beards and frosty hair,
But when we go and hunt for him,
   He isn't anywhere!

"Nature is painting for us, day after day, pictures of
infinite beauty." – John Ruskin

## THE CREATION

Berdice Moran (1884-1969,) published in
*Verses for Tiny Tots*, 1937

In heaven, up above
Dwells the Father, God of love.
He made the earth; He made the sky,
The ocean wide, the mountains high,
He made each flower and bird and tree,
He made you, and He made me.
He sends the snow; He sends the rain;
He makes the flowers bloom again,
And when the earth is bleak and bare,
He feeds the birdies everywhere.

"For out of ourselves we can never pass, nor can
there be in creation what in the Creator was not."
Oscar Wilde

## HEARTS WERE MADE TO GIVE AWAY

Annette Wynne (died 1953), published in
*For Days and Days*, 1919

Hearts were made to give away
On St. Valentine's good day;
Wrap them up in dainty white,
Send them off the thirteenth night,
Any kind of heart that's handy—
Hearts of lace and hearts of candy,
Hearts all trimmed with ribbons fine
Send for good St. Valentine.
Hearts were made to give away
On St. Valentine's dear day.

"The love of silence leads to the silence of love."
St. Elizabeth of the Trinity

February 14
St. Valentine's Day

## MY VALENTINE
Mary Catherine Parsons, published in "The Youth's
Companion", Volume 91, January 4, 1917

I have a little valentine
    That someone sent to me.
It's pink and white and red and blue,
    And pretty as can be.

Forget-me-nots are round the edge,
    And tiny roses, too;
And such a lovely piece of lace—
    The very palest blue.

And in the center there's a heart,
    As red as red can be!
And on it's written all in gold,
    "To YOU, with love from ME."

"Keep close to Nature's heart." – John Muir

## BIRDIE'S VALENTINE
Sophia Bixby, published in
*Primary Education: Volume 4*, 1896

In the sunny Southland,
Where the trees are green,
And the orange blossoms
All the year are seen:
Sang a bright-eyed birdie
In the spring sunshine,
"Dear Miss Robin Redbreast,
Be my valentine."

So they journeyed northward,
Dressed in red and brown;
Build a cozy bird's nest
In a quiet town.
There they lived all summer
'Neath a climbing vine—
Gallant Robin Redbreast
And his valentine.

"Saint Bonaventure teaches us that 'contemplation
deepens the more we feel the working of God's
grace within our hearts, and the better we learn to
encounter God in creatures outside ourselves.'"
*Laudato Si'* 233

February 16

## THE FALLING SNOW
Published in *Our Little Tot's Speaker*, 1899

Oh, see! The snow
Is falling now—
It powders all the trees.
Its flakes abound,
And all around
They float upon the breeze.

'Tis snowing fast,
And cold the blast;
But yet I hope 'twill stay;—
Oh, see it blow,
The falling snow,
In shadows far away.

Jack Frost is here—
We feel him near—
He's on his icy sled.
And covered deep,
The flowers sleep
Beneath their snowy bed.

Come out and play
This wintry day,
Amidst the falling snow;
Come, young and old,
Fear not the cold,
Nor howling winds that blow.

"As he that fears God, fears nothing else; so he that
sees God, sees everything else." – John Donne

## MY LITTLE STAR

Annette Wynne (died 1953), published in
*For Days and Days*, 1919

My little star lives very high;
I almost lose it in the sky,
Because there are so many others,
Sisters, cousins, aunts and brothers;
All beside it looking down
In the windows of our town;
But my star is mine alone,
I shall keep it for my own,
Keep it where it lives so high
In its corner of the sky;
Other children, take the rest,
This small star I'll love the best.

"A gleam of heaven; the passion of a star
Held captive in the clasp of harmony;
A silence, shell-like, breathing from afar
The rapture of the deep—eternity."
John B. Tabb

## CRUMBS TO THE BIRDS
Charles Lamb (1775-1834), published in
*Poetry for Children*, 1903

A bird appears a thoughtless thing,
He's ever living on the wing,
And keeps up such a caroling,
That little else to do but sing
    A man would guess had he.

No doubt he has his little cares,
And very hard he often fares,
The which so patiently he bears,
That, listening to those cheerful airs,
    Who knows but he may be

In want of his next meal of seeds?
I think for that his sweet song pleads.
If so, his pretty art succeeds.
I'll scatter there among the weeds
    All the small crumbs I see.

"The bee with his comb,
The mouse at her dray,
The grub in his tomb,
Wile winter away;
But the fire-fly and hedge-shrew, and lob-worm, I pray,
How are they . . . ?" – Robert Browning

## PLAYGROUNDS
Laurence Alma-Tadema (1836-1912),
published in *Songs of Womanhood*, 1903

In summer I am very glad
We children are so small,
For we can see a thousand things
That men can't see at all.

They don't know much about the moss
And all the stones they pass:
They never lie and play among
The forests in the grass:

They walk about a long way off;
And, when we're at the sea,
Let father stoop as best he can
He can't find things like me.

But, when the snow is on the ground
And all the puddles freeze,
I wish that I were very tall,
High up above the trees. . . .

"The question is not what you look at,
but what you see." – Henry David Thoreau

### SNOW DUST
Robert Frost (1874-1963),
published in *Yale Review*, 1921

The way a crow

Shook down on me
The dust of snow
From a hemlock tree

Has given my heart
A change of mood
And saved some part
Of a day I had rued.


### HAPPY THOUGHT
Robert Louis Stevenson (1850-1894), published in
*A Child's Garden of Verses*, 1885

The world is so full

of a number of things,
I'm sure we should all be
As happy as kings.


"A single crow on the tree-top bleak
From his shining feathers sheds off the cold sun."
James Russell Lowell

## THE STARS' BALL
Jessie Burweil, published in
"Ladies Home Journal: Volume 8", 1891

OH! The stars, one and all,
   They had a great ball
   One night, way up in the sky;
They invited the Earth
To join in their mirth,
     But it feared to go up so high.

No fiddler had they
Their music to play,
     And the stars were afraid 'twould fail;
But the man in the moon
He whistled a tune,
     And the comet kept time with his tail.

They danced, and they danced,
And they pranced, and they pranced,
     Till the Moon said 'twas all he desired
For his lips were so sore
He could whistle no more,
     And the comet began to get tired.

So they faded away
In the dim light of day,
     The moon and the stars from the ball.
But sad to relate,
Next night they were late,
     And came near not shining at all.

"Hitch your wagon to a star."
Ralph Waldo Emerson

## THE CATHOLIC CHURCH

Sister Mary Josita Belger (1899-1978),
published in *Sing a Song of Holy Things*, 1945

I love our holy Catholic Church
Our saintly Church of Rome.
I like to pray for it each day.
And keep it for a home.

Our Savior made Saint Peter head
Of this great church of ours.
He gave him keys to open and lock,
He gave him many powers.

And every Pope in Peter's chair
Can do these very things,
And helped by all the holy priests,
God's loving grace now brings.

Our Savior made His holy Church
To show His love for man.
How glad I am to be its child.
I'll serve it all I can.

"'And so I say to you, you are Peter, and upon this
rock I will build my church, and the gates of the
netherworld shall not prevail against it.'"
Matthew 16:18

## SYMPATHY
Published in *A Jolly Jingle-Book*, 1913

Sometimes the world's asleep so soon
When all the winds are still,
That I can see the little moon
Come peeping o'er the hill.

It looks so small and scared and white,
The way I feel in bed
When I have just put out the light
And covered up my head.

It half seems wishing it had stayed,
And half creeps softly out.
"Dear moon," I say, "don't be afraid!
No bogies are about."


## LIGHT NIGHT
Published in *The Lore and Language
of Schoolchildren*, 1967

There's no need to light a night light
On a light night like tonight
For a night light's a slight light
On a light night like tonight.


"I have loved the stars too fondly to be
fearful of the night." – Sarah Williams

## THE LADY MOON
Alice Turner Curtis 1860-1958), published in
*A Jolly Jingle-Book*, 1913

There's a lady in the moon,

With a floating gown of white;
You can see her very soon,
When mamma turns out the light.

'Tis a lady and she smiles
Through my narrow window way,
As she sails on miles and miles,
Making night as fair as day.

## THE MAN IN THE MOON
Published in *Weather Opinions*, 1907

The man in the moon

Who sails through the sky,
Is a most courageous skipper;
Yet he made a mistake
When he first tried to take
A drink of milk from the Dipper.
He dipped it into the "Milky Way,"
And slowly, cautiously filled it;
The Great Bear growled,
And the Little Bear howled;
And scared him so much that he spilled it.

"Come forth into the light of things; let nature be your
teacher." – William Wordsworth

February 25

## BEDTIME
E. H. T., published in
*School Education: Volume 17*, 1898

# Do you know
Why the snow
Is hurrying through the garden so?
Just to spread
A nice soft bed
For the sleepy little flower's head;
To cover up the baby ferns and smooth the lily's
sheet,
And tuck a warm white blanket down around the
rose's feet.

## BEYOND WINTER
(FROM "THE WORLD-SOUL")
Ralph Waldo Emerson (1803-1882),
published in *Poems*, 1847

# Over the winter glaciers
I see the summer glow,
And through the wild-piled snowdrift
The warm rosebuds below.

"When one tugs at a single thing in nature, he finds it
attached to the rest of the world." – John Muir

## CALENDAR OF A COUNTRY CHILD
Alice Van Leer Carrick (1875-1961),
published in *In Playland*, 1911

Such splendid things I think and do,
The whole year round, the long year through!
In January are skates and sled
And blazing fires with birch logs fed.
In February are swift sleigh-rides,
And corn to pop and nuts besides.
With March's lively, slushy snow
I build my dikes and dams, you know;
And April weather, chill and cold,
Gives me gray catkins soft to hold.
Blue May is kind to little girls
And shakes me dandelion curls;
And dear June twines white daisy-chains,
While robins chirp in soft, warm rains.
In green July I rest so still,
Where clover carpets all the hill;
And where the clear brook slips away
In August days I wade and play.
And when September's harvests come
I ride on creaking wagons home.
October throws me fruit to hold
Like bits of sunset, red and gold.
I shake and shake the chestnuts down,
When all November's woods are brown.
And last, December's snow drifts white
To make me happy Christmas night.

The whole year round, the whole year through,
Such splendid things I think and do!

"At times on quiet waters one does not speak aloud
but only in whispers, for then all noise is sacrilege."
Sigurd Olson

## I DUG AND DUG AMONGST THE SNOW
Christina Rossetti (1830-1894),
published in *Sing Song, A Nursery Rhyme Book*, 1872

I dug and dug amongst the snow,
And thought the flowers would never grow;
I dug and dug amongst the sand,
And still no green thing came to hand.

Melt, O snow! The warm winds blow
To thaw the flowers and melt the snow;
But all the winds from every land
Will rear no blossom from the sand.

"February makes a bridge, and March breaks it."
George Herbert

## NORTHERN LIGHTS
B. F. Taylor, published in
*Young Folks Book of Poetry*, 1880

To claim the Arctic came the sun
With banners of the burning zone,—
Unrolled upon their airy spars,
They froze beneath the light of stars;
And there they float, those streamers old,
Those Northern Lights, forever cold.

"When you see the aurora, the only logical choice
you can make is to spend this rest of your life seeking
the sublime." – Ken Ilgunas, *Walden on Wheels*

## LEAP YEAR

Annette Wynne (died 1953), published in
*For Days and Days*, 1919

Little month of February,
You are small, but worthy—very!
Will you grow up like the others,
Like your sister months and brothers?
Every four years with a bound
With a leap up from the ground,
Trying to grow tall as they—
All you stretch is one small day!
Even then you're not so tall
But just the shortest month of all.

"With divine recompense
he comes to save you. . . .
Then the lame shall leap like a stag,
and the mute tongue sing for joy." – Isaiah 35:4, 6

# HOLY DAYS AND HOLIDAYS

## A CHRISTMAS GREETING

Cascia, published in *"Ave Maria"* magazine,
December 25, 1909

Dear little Christ Child, on this day
  Which gladdens every heart,
I hope in all our happiness
  You, too, will have a part.

A merry Christmas, little King,
  And gifts the kind You love—
Sweet deeds of tender charity
  Done for our God above.

For Mother Mary, too, I send
  A Christmas greeting true.
What happiness must fill her heart!
  Her Christmas joy is you!

And dear St. Joseph, guardian blest,
  So faithful in his care—
In all our happy Christmas thoughts
  He, too, must have a share.

A merry Christmas! Carols ring
  With joy from shore to shore,
A happy birthday, little King,
  And many, many more!

## LITTLE CHILD'S PRAYER
(Before the Christmas Crib)
Hyacinth Blocker (1904-1969), published in
*Locust Bloom and Other Poems*, 1938

Lady, by the manger,
Hear my little prayer,
Kneeling by the manger
With Him lying there,
Lying in the manger
Rosy-white and fair.

I would love to play here
With your Little Son,
Tumble in the hay here
Just to give Him fun,
Dance and sing and stay here
Till the day is done. . . .

Lady, by the manger,
Hear this little prayer,
Kneeling by the manger
With Him lying there,
Lying in the manger
Smiling, sweet and fair.

## CHILD AT THE CRIB
Mary Mabel Wirries (1893-1967), published in
*Gay Witch April and Other Poems*, 1936

Sleepily I've followed far,
Little Baby God.
The sweet shining of your star,
Little Baby God.
And at last I've found you here,
With Mary and Joseph near.
Oh! But you are small and dear,
Little Baby God.

I am just a child like You,
Little Baby God.
But I heard the Angels, too,
Little Baby God.
Heard them singing in the skies,
Heard them bid the shepherds rise.
Like the Kings, I, too, am wise,
Little Baby God.

Oh, the night is cold and cruel,
Little Baby God.
In the stable there's no fuel,
Little Baby God.
Let my heart be kind and warm,
Let me shield You from the storm,
Let my love keep You from harm,
Little Baby God.

## "X" IS FOR XMAS

Hilda van Stockum (1908-2006), published in
*Angels' Alphabet*, 1948

**"X"** used to be the Greek letter for Christ
And in Xmas it's written so yet
Putting across in the happy word
Like a shade over Christ's bassinet.

"X" is also the symbol for what is unknown
And no one knew Him at all
Who was expected with royal pomp
And came as a babe in a stall.

I only wish I had lived that day
And heard the angels' song.
I would have hurried across the hills
Bringing my toys along.

I would have hurried across the hills
Wherever the big star led,
To kneel down at the baby's feet
And give Him all I had.

## A CHILD'S SONG OF CHRISTMAS
Marjorie L. C. Pickthall (1883-1922),
published in *The Drift of Pinions*, 1913

My counterpane* is soft as silk,
My blankets white as creamy milk.
    The hay was soft to Him, I know,
    Our little Lord of long ago.

Above the roofs the pigeons fly
In silver wheels across the sky.
    The stable-doves they cooed to them,
    Mary and Christ in Bethlehem.

Bright shines the sun across the drifts,
And bright upon my Christmas gifts.
    They brought Him incense, myrrh, and gold,
    Our little Lord who lived of old.

Oh, soft and clear our mother sings
Of Christmas joys and Christmas things.
    God's holy angels sang to them,
    Mary and Christ in Bethlehem.

Our hearts they hold all Christmas dear,
And earth seems sweet and heaven seems near.
    Oh, heaven was in His sight, I know,
    That little Child of long ago.


*Bedspread; quilt

## THE SHEPHERDS ON THE HILL
Sister Mary Josita Belger (1899-1978),
published in *Sing a Song of Holy Things*, 1945

On a green and quiet hillside
Many, many years ago,
Flocks of sheep were eating slowly,
Moving, moving to and fro.

Oh, the quiet of that valley
As the shining stars looked down.
Little knew the tired shepherds
The great wonder of the town.

As they lay there almost sleeping,
Suddenly a light came forth,
Filling all the sky with glory,
Shining bright from south to north.

Then an angel told the story
Of the little Savior's birth,
How He rested in a manger
When He came from heaven to earth.

Angel voices filled the heavens—
"In excelsis gloria!"
As the shepherds looked with wonder—
"In excelsis gloria!"

## SONG

Eugene Field (1850-1895), published in
*The Poems of Eugene Field*, 1916

Why do bells for Christmas ring?
Why do little children sing?

Once a lovely, shining star,
Seen by shepherds from afar,
Gently moved until its light
Made a manger's cradle bright.

There a darling baby lay,
Pillowed soft upon the hay;
And its mother sang and smiled,
"This is Christ, the holy Child!"

Therefore bells for Christmas ring,
Therefore little children sing.

## LONG, LONG AGO
Published in "Young Citizen:
A Magazine for Supplemental Reading", 1904

Winds through the olive trees
Softly did blow
Round little Bethlehem
Long, long ago.

Sheep on the hillside lay
White as the snow;
Shepherds were watching them,
Long, long ago.

Then from the happy skies,
Angels bent low,
Singing their songs of joy,
Long, long ago.

For in His manger bed
Cradled, we know,
Christ came to Bethlehem,
Long, long ago.

# A CHRISTMAS CAROL

G. .K. Chesterton (1874-1936), published in
"The Expository Times: Volume 19", 1908

The Christ-child lay on Mary's lap,
  His hair was like a light.
(O weary, weary were the world,
  But here is all aright.)

The Christ-child lay on Mary's breast,
  His hair was like a star.
(O stern and cunning are the kings,
  But here the true hearts are.)

The Christ-child lay on Mary's heart,
  His hair was like a fire.
(O weary, weary is the world,
  But here the world's desire.)

The Christ-child stood at Mary's knee,
  His hair was like a crown.
And all the flowers looked up at Him,
  And all the stars looked down.

## WHAT LOVELY INFANT CAN THIS BE
Frederick William Faber (1814-1863), published in
*Course of Christian Doctrine:*
*A Handbook for Teachers*, 1904

**W**hat lovely Infant can this be
That in the little crib I see?
So sweetly on the straw it lies,
It must have come from Paradise.

## MY GIFT
### (FROM "A CHRISTMAS CAROL")
Christina Rossetti (1830-1894), published in *The*
*Poetical Works of Christina Georgina Rossetti*, 1906

**W**hat can I give Him
Poor as I am?
If I were a shepherd
I would bring a lamb.
If I were a Wise Man,
I would do my part.
Yet what can I give Him?
Give Him my heart.

# GIFTS

Julia Johnson Davis, published in
*Religious Poems for Little Folks*, 1936

The shepherds brought a little lamb
    To lie beside Him there,
The shepherds brought their softest wood,
    Do we bring nothing fair?

The Wise Men brought Him gold and myrrh
    And frankincense so sweet
But only the rich can hope to lay
    Such treasures at His feet.

Poor, yet we can bring Him one gift
    Who comes from heaven above,
Better than lamb or gold or myrrh,
    And that is *love*.

Feast of the Epiphany
Sunday between January 2 and January 8

# THE EPIPHANY
Emily Henrietta Hickey (1845-1923),
published in *Later Poems*, 1913

Three kings went upon their way,
To find a mightier King than they.

Three wise men, with heaven-taught eyes,
Looked for the Wisest of the wise.

The mighty ones to their Mightier
Brought gold and frankincense and myrrh.

The wise knelt to the Wisest One;
Their star had led them to the Sun.

The grown kings had their joy complete
Low at a little Child-King's feet.

All the way the kings had trod,
Seeking a King, and finding God.

Little King, greatest King,
Unto Thee our hearts we bring.

## SAINT JOSEPH

Rev Hugh F. Blunt (1877-1957), published in
*A Lovely Gate Set Wide,* 1946

Three Wise Men came, their gifts to bring

Unto the little new-born King;
Gold, frankincense, and myrrh they gave,
Making His crib a treasure cave.
Happy were they to make Him glad;
Such gifts, they thought, He never had.

They little guessed that Joseph, poor,
Had brought such very gifts before,
A heart of gold, incense of prayer,
And myrrh of all the pains he bare.
Good Wise Men, see a wiser one,
Who calls the God ye worship—Son!

# THE BAPTISM: MATTHEW 3:1-17
Janet P. McKenzie

The preacher, the locusts, the camel's hair too,
He came from the desert, the crowds larger grew:
"Repent, for the Kingdom of God is at hand."
Baptism of water, good fruit to demand.

The Baptist, the river, the water, the Son,
Fulfillment of righteousness, job to be done:
"You know I'm not worthy to do this," he said.
But Jesus insisted, and John went ahead.

The Spirit, the opening, the Dove coming near,
A Voice from the heavens, the message quite clear:
"I am well-pleased with Him, My Beloved Son."
His fasting now over; His mission begun.

The fighting, the sinners, the world gone astray,
For their sins—for my sins—our Savior must pay.
"Father, forgive them. They know not what they do."
His mercy flows freely our hope to renew.

The preaching, the healing, forgiveness of sins,
from Baptism to Calvary, our freedom He wins.
"I thirst." Will you comfort Him? Accept His grace?
Let His mercy enfold you—His love embrace.

## UNPLANNED CHILD
Janet P. McKenzie

The angel's voice,
And Mary's choice,
Then Joseph's doubt—
Not opting out;
As guided in dreamland.

On Christmas morn
The Child was born.
Not prince, not king,
Not anything
That showed His Father's Hand.

But by this child
We're reconciled—
The human race
Now saved by grace
Due to this babe unplanned.

Each child is dear,
Its mission clear
To God who cares
For all His heirs—
His law of love should stand.

Each child protect,
Do not neglect
To pray each day
To change the way
Of law within our land.

## THE LAND WHERE HATE SHOULD DIE
Denis A. McCarthy (1871-1931), published in
*Heart Songs and Home Songs*, 1916

This is the land where hate should die—
  No feuds of faith, no spleen of race,
No darkly brooding fear should try
  Beneath our flag to find a place.
Lo! Every people here has sent
  Its sons to answer freedom's call;
Their lifeblood is the strong cement
  That builds and binds the nation's wall.

This is the land where hate should die—
  Though dear to me my faith and shrine,
I serve my country well when I
  Respect the creeds that are not mine.
He little loves his land who'd cast
  Upon his neighbor's word a doubt,
Or cite the wrongs of ages past
  From present rights to bar him out.

This is the land where hate should die—
  This is the land where strife should cease,
Where foul, suspicious fear should fly
  Before the light of love and peace.
Then let us purge from poisoned thought
  That service to the state we give,
And so be worthy as we ought
  Of this great land in which we live!

# LINCOLN

[Traditionally celebrated February 12]

Ella Wheeler Wilcox (1850-1919), published in
*Sailing Sunny Seas*, 1909

When God created this good world,
A few stupendous peaks were hurled
From His strong hand, and they remain
The wonder of the level plain.
But these colossal heights are rare,
While shifting sands are everywhere.

So with the race. The centuries pass,
And nations fall like leaves of grass.
They die, forgotten and unsung.
While straight from God some souls are flung
To live immortal and sublime.
So lives great Lincoln for all time.

## WASHINGTON'S BIRTHDAY
[Traditionally celebrated February 22]

Margaret Elizabeth Sangster (1838-1912), published in
*Child's Calendar Beautiful*, 1906

'T is splendid to live so grandly
That long after you are gone,
The things you did are remembered,
And recounted under the sun;
To live so bravely and purely,
That a nation stops on its way,
And once a year, with banner and drum,
Keeps its thought of your natal day. . . .

And this is Washington's glory,
A steadfast soul and true,
Who stood for his country's honor
When his country's days were few.
And now when its days are many,
And its flag of stars is flung
To the breeze in defiant challenge,
His name is on every tongue.

# ASH WEDNESDAY AND LENT

# ASH WEDNESDAY (1862)

Fr. Abram Joseph Ryan (1838-1886), published in
*War Lyrics and Songs of the South*, 1866

T he six weeks' Sabbath has begun;
A little while, my soul be done
With heat and flurry of life's race;
Take time to cultivate God's grace.

Most of the seeds He sowed are lost,
Those that are left are passion-tost:
Save them, heart, ere it be too late;
Redeem them from pride, scorn, and hate. . . .

Thy Father knows is best for thee:
Trust Him, for farther He can see
Than thou. Think of thy love-marked past—
Easter comes after Lenten fast. . . .

## WISHING
Ella Wheeler Wilcox (1855-1919), published in
*Poems of Power*, 1902

Do you wish the world were better?
Let me tell you what to do:
Set a watch upon your actions,
Keep them always straight and true;
Let your thoughts be clean and high:
Of the sphere you occupy.

Do you wish the world was wiser?
Well, suppose you make a start
By accumulating wisdom
In the scrapbook of your heart.
Do not waste one page on folly;
Live to learn, and learn to live.
If you want to give men knowledge
You must get it ere you give.

Do you wish the world were happy?
Then remember day by day
Just to scatter seeds of kindness
As you pass along the way:
For the pleasures of many
May be oft times traced to one,
As the hand that plants an acorn
Shelters armies from the sun.

## THE CATHOLIC CHILD
Sister Mary Josita Belger (1899-1978), published in
*Sing a Song of Holy Things*, 1945

A good and holy child of God
A child of Mother Church
Is known by how he acts each day
You need not stop to search.

He goes to Mass on Sundays
And all the Holy Days,
And shows that he is serving God
In many little ways.

He eats no meat on Fridays,
But takes a fish instead.
He gives up for his Savior,
And still he is well fed.

He loves the holy sacraments—
Confession for his sins,
Communion with his Savior
Heaven's joy on earth begins.

You always know a child of God,
He's happy as can be.
Because he keeps the holy law
Of Mother Church, you see.

## AFTER A VISIT TO THE BLESSED SACRAMENT
S.M. St. John, published in
*Religious Poems for Little Folks*, 1936

Whenever in pain or sin,
I love to enter in
Before some altar door,
God's favor to implore.

We talk a little while—
A word or two, a smile,
His love's absolving kiss,
Such reverential bliss!

And then with clearer ken
I face life's ways again;
'Mid all its deafening roar,
King of my soul once more!

## GOD'S GREATNESS
Sister Mary Josita Belger (1899-1978), published in
*Sing a Song of Holy Things*, 1945

Dear God, I know You're everywhere
No matter where I go, you're there.

If I could fly above the sky,
Your throne would be there built on high.

And if I dig down in the ground,
Even there You're to be found.

Wherever there's a single space
The angels see You face to face.

But I can't see You till I die—
No matter how hard I may try.

For You are spirit; You can see,
And know all things—yes, even me.

You know my thoughts, my words, my deeds,
Your loving eye sees all my needs.

There's nothing hard for You to do;
To make a world is fun for You.

You take the good to heaven bright,
And punish evil with Your might.

But You are patient, kind, and true
To sinners who come back to You.

Your holiness I now adore,
Oh, make me love You more and more.

## MORNING PRAYER
John C. Rath (1910-2007), published in
*Religious Poems for Little Folks*, 1936

Jesus, your child returns to You

The many thanks that are Your due;
All that I think, or do, or say
Give praise to you throughout the day.

Angel of God, your vigil kept
Beside my bed, the while I slept;
Keep me from sin and guide aright
that I may follow pathways bright.

Mother of God, forever true,
Your little one now calls on you;
Grant me to live like your dear Son,
To be with you when life is done. Amen.

## A SIMPLE RECIPE
### James Whitcomb Riley (1849-1916), published in
*Joyful Poems for Children*, 1892

To be a wholly worthy man,
As you, my boy, would like to be,—
This is to show you how you can—
This simple recipe:

Be honest—both in word and act,
Be strictly truthful through and through:
Fact cannot fail. You stick to fact,
And fact will stick to you.

Be clean—outside and in, and sweep
Both hearth and heart and hold them bright;
Wear snowy linen—aye, and keep
Your *conscience* snowy-white.

Do right, your utmost—good *must come*
To you who do your level-best—
Your very hopes will help you some,
And work will do the rest.

## HYMN TO THE HOLY CHILD JESUS
Published in *Pleadings of the Soul*, 1895

Jesus, teach me how to pray,

Suffer not my thoughts to stray,
Send distractions far away,
Sweet Holy Child.

Let me not be rude or wild,
Make me humble, meek, and mild,
Pure as angels undefiled,
Sweet Holy Child.

When I work, or when I play,
Be Thou with me through the day,
Teach me what to do and say,
Sweet Holy Child.

Make me love Thy Mother blest,
Safe beneath her care to rest,
As a bird within its nest,
Sweet Holy Child.

## LITTLE THINGS
Julia Fletcher Carney, 1823-1908,
published in *The Home Book of Verse*, 1915

Little drops of water,
Little grains of sand,
Make the mighty ocean
And the pleasant land.

Thus the little minutes
Humble though they be,
Make the mighty ages
Of eternity.

Thus our little errors
Lead the soul away
From the path of virtue
Off in sin to stray.

## THE WAY OF THE CROSS
Leonard Feeney (1897-1978), published in
*In Towns and Little Towns*, 1927

Along the dark aisles

Of a chapel dim,
The little lame girl
Drags her withered limb.

And all alone she searches
The shadows on the walls
To find the three pictures
Where Jesus falls.

## WHAT GOD HATH MADE

William Bourne Oliver Peabody (1799-1847), published
in *Bancroft's First-Fifth Reader: Book 3*, 1883

God made the sun, and gave him light;
He made the moon to shine by night;
He placed the brilliant stars on high,
And leads them through the midnight sky.

He made the earth in order stand;
He made the ocean and the land;
He made the hills their places know,
And gentle rivers round them flow.

He made the forests, and sustains
The grass that clothes the field and plains;
He sends from heaven the summer showers,
And makes the meadows bright with flowers.

He made the living things; with care
He feeds the wanderers of the air;
He gave the beasts their dens and caves,
And fish, their dwelling in the waves.

He called all beings into birth
That crowd the ocean, air, and earth;
And all in heaven and earth proclaim
The glory of His holy name.

## LOVE AT HOME

Sister Mary Josita Belger (1899-1978),
published in *Sing a Song of Holy Things*, 1945

Home is a very happy place
When all begin the day
With prayer to ask God's blessing
And help along the way,

When children honor, love, obey,
And share their every toy,
Are always kind in thought and deed
And give their parents joy.

When all the family kneel at night
To say an evening prayer,
To thank God for His blessings
And for His loving care.

Such homes are lovely gardens
Where God can walk each day,
Where flowers give sweet perfumes
Along the Master's way.

## DO NOT LOOK FOR WRONG OR EVIL
Alice Cary (1820-1871), published in *The Poetical Works of Alice and Phoebe Cary*, 1884

**D**o not look for wrong and evil—
You will find them if you do;
As you measure for your neighbor
He will measure back to you.

Look for goodness, look for gladness,
You will meet them all the while;
If you bring a smiling visage
To the glass, you meet a smile.

## THE HIGHEST GOOD

James Whitcomb Riley (1849-1916),
published in *Joyful Poems for Children*, 1892

To attain the highest good

Of true man and womanhood,
Simply do your honest best—
God with joy will do the rest.

## TRY AGAIN

William Hickson (1803-1870), published in
"Supplement to the Courant: Volume 6," 1840

'Tis a lesson you should heed—
    Try again;
If at first you don't succeed,
    Try again.
Then your courage should appear;
For if you will persevere,
You will conquer, never fear,
    Try again.

Once or twice though you should fail,
If you would at last prevail,
    Try again.
If we strive, 'tis no disgrace
Though we did not win the race—
What should you do in that case?
    Try again.

If you find your task is hard.
    Try again;
Time will bring you your reward,
    Try again;
All that other folk can do,
Why with patience should not you?
Only keep this rule in view,
    Try again.

## GOD'S HOME [ADAPTED]
Rev. Edward F. Garesche (1876-1960),
published in *The Four Gates*, 1913

"Mother, where does Jesus dwell?"
Child, He dwells everywhere,
In the earth and in the air,
In the wide, unending blue—
Even on the farthest star,
Where creation's lights are,
Past all ken* of me and you!

"Mother, has He any home?"
First, His home's in heaven bright,
Wondrous mansions, built of light;
Then, the tabernacle blest;
But the home He loves the most,
More than heaven or Sacred Host,
Is your sinless, loving breast!

* range of knowledge; understanding

## HOW TO BE HAPPY
Published in *Child's Calendar Beautiful*, 1905

Are you cross and disgusted, my dear little man?
　　I will tell you a wonderful trick
That will bring you contentment if anything can:
　　　　Do something for somebody—quick!
　　　　Do something for somebody—quick!

Are you very tired with play, little girl?
　　Weary, discouraged, and sick?
I'll tell you the loveliest game in the world—
　　　　Do something for somebody—quick!
　　　　Do something for somebody—quick!

Though it rain like the rain of the floods, little man,
　　And the clouds are forbidding and thick,
You can make the sun shine in your soul, little
man—
　　　　Do something for somebody—quick!
　　　　Do something for somebody—quick!

Though the skies are like brass overhead, little girl,
　　And the walk like a well-heated brick;
And are all your affairs in a terrible whirl?
　　　　Do something for somebody—quick!
　　　　Do something for somebody—quick!

## OBEDIENCE
Phoebe Cary (1824-1871), published in
*The Poetical Works of Alice and Phoebe Cary*, 1884

If you're told to do a thing,

And mean to do it really;
Never let it be by halves;
Do it fully, freely!

Do not make a poor excuse,
Waiting, weak, unsteady;
All obedience worth the name,
Must be prompt and ready.

## THE TEN COMMANDMENTS
Sister Mary Josita Belger (1899-1978), published in
*Sing a Song of Holy Things*, 1945

The First Commandment says that I should pray to
God alone.
And love Him more than anything I think, or see, or own.
The Second one commands us all to bless the Holy Name,
Not speak It when we're angry, not in fun—'twould be a
shame.
The Third Commandment tells us all to keep the Lord's
day well,
To go to Mass, to do kind acts, and other prayers to tell.
The Fourth reminds us all to love our parents and obey,
That God may bless us while on earth in every little way.
The Fifth Commandment tells us we must not kill anyone,
Not harm a person any way, no matter how it's done.
The Sixth and Ninth Commandments tells us always to
be pure,
And then we'll all be happy and will make our heaven
secure.
The Seventh says we may not steal from any one at all,
And if we borrow, give it back—a crayon or a ball.
The Eighth Commandment warns that we should never
tell a lie,
Nor say mean things of others, though they have made
us cry.
And by the Tenth and last command God wants us all to
be
Happy with what we have and own, not wishing all we see.
And if we keep these ten commands that God gave us on
stone,
We show Him that we want to live for Him, for Him alone.

## GOD'S HELP

Sister Mary Josita Belger (1899-1978),
published in *Sing a Song of Holy Things*, 1945

God is very near each day,
So when I work or when I play
I say, "My Jesus, help!"

Just as soon as I awake,
And promise things for His dear sake,
I add, "My Jesus, help!"

Whenever hard things come my way,
I always stop and quickly say,
"My Lord, my Jesus, help!"

Jesus hears me when I call;
He gives His helping grace to all
Who say, "My Jesus help!"

## EVERY DAY

Felix Mendelssohn (1809-1847),
published in *Stories of Great Musicians*, 1905

L ove the beautiful,

Seek out the true,
Wish for the good,
And the best do!

(See Philippians 4:8)

## DON'T GIVE UP
Phoebe Cary (1824-1871), published in
*The Poetical Works of Alice and Phoebe Cary*, 1884

If you've tried and have not won,
Never stop for crying;
All that's great and good is done
Just by patient trying.

Though young birds, in flying, fall,
Still their wings grow stronger;
And the next time they can keep
Up a little longer.

Though the sturdy oak has known
Many a blast that bowed her,
She has risen again, and grown
Loftier and prouder.

If by easy work you beat,
Who the more will prize you?
Gaining victory from defeat,
That's the test that tries you!

# First Friday and
# First Saturday
# Meditations

## BEGGARS

Hyacinth Blocker (1904-1969), published in
*Locust Bloom and Other Poems*, 1938

Beggars are we
  Who knock at your gate,
Lone beggars, Lord,
  Who sit and who wait
To catch the choice crumbs
  That fall from Your Table.
(To live of ourselves
  We, Lord, are unable.)
And so all the day
  We but gaze on your Face
And beg for the crumbs—
  The crumbs of Your grace.


(See Matthew 15:21-28.)

## THE HAIL MARY

Marigold Hunt (1905-1994), published in
*Gospel Rhymes*, 1947

Our Lady helped her mother
To wash the breakfast things,
  And in the garden Gabriel
  Waited, with folded wings.
Our Lady came to the garden
  For lettuces and peas,
And Gabriel knelt to worship her
  Humbly, on his knees.

Our Lady's soul was shining
The light was in her face—
*"Hail, full of grace,"* said Gabriel,
*"Hail, full of grace."*

He began a prayer
For you and me,
*"Hail, Mary, full of grace
The Lord is with thee."*

## PEACE
T. V. Nicholas, published in *Gospel Rhymes*, 1947

We mustn't fret and fear, because Our Lord Himself
　has said:
"Let not your heart be troubled not let it be afraid."
The cripple at Bethsaida couldn't even find a friend
To put him in the water when the angel should descend.

This angel moved the waters and he healed the first
　man in.
It seemed a competition that our cripple couldn't win.
But since he waited patiently and wouldn't give up heart,
God gave the winner's prize to one who hadn't taken part.

He told Saint Martha not to cook all sorts of extra things,
He told us not to worry about what tomorrow brings,
And if at time we're puzzled, yet we never must forget,
He's making any plans for us we can't imagine yet.

*Dear Lord, You left Your peace with us; I think You left*
　*it here*
*That we might keep it in our hearts to keep out fret or fear.*

(See John 5:5-15.)

## OUR LADY'S VISIT

Father Cheerheart, published in
*"Ave Maria"* magazine, July 3, 1909

When Mary, prompt to do God's will,
Sped swiftly over vale and hill,
Her loving mission to fulfill
   Toward Saint Elizabeth,
The grasses bowed themselves full low,
Midsummer blooms made haste to blow,
And gladsome breezes whispered low
   "Hail Mary" with each breath.

And oft as we, like Mary, speed
To do a kindly, loving deed,
There greet us, though we take no heed,
   Fair tribute from above.
Our Guardian Angels rapture show,
Our Lady's mien* with joy doth glow,
And o'er us streams of graces flow
   From Christ, the Fount of love.


* appearance; look; expression

## FOLLOW THOU ME
### Annie Johnson Flint (1866-1932)

Follow—not go ahead at thine own pleasure,

Nor turn aside at thine own wayward will,
Nor stray afar in search of other treasure,
But close at hand, where I can aid thee still;
Across the sea and through the desert places,
Onward and upward by the one sure way,
Till thou shalt sit with me in heavenly places
Amid the splendors of eternal day. . . .

Follow thou me—though stranger voices hail thee,
I am the way and there is none beside;
There is no other staff that shall not fail thee,
There is no other eye than mine to guide;
There is no other shepherd who can fold thee
By such still waters, in such pastures fair;
There is no other arm can safely hold thee
In doubt and danger, darkness and despair.

Trust me to lead thee home to God and heaven;
What others do or say is naught to thee;
No other light, no other truth, is given;
Follow—follow thou—follow me.

## BETHLEHEM
T. V. Nicholas, published in *Gospel Rhymes*, 1947

The Shepherds found the Holy Babe,

His bed was prickly straw,
His Mother and Saint Joseph
Bad them enter and adore.
The shepherds knelt before Him,
Roughly clad and roughly shod,
And when they touched his baby hands
They felt the strength of God.

*Baby Jesus, oh so tiny,*
*All tied up in swaddling bands,*
*Draw us with your love almighty*
*Hold us with your baby hands.*

## HIDE AND SEEK
Fr. John Tabb (1845-1909),
published in *Child Verse*, 1899

You hid your little self, dear Lord,

As other children do;
But oh, how great was their reward
Who sought three days for You!

# ADDITIONAL RESOURCES

## WHO HATH A BOOK
Wilbur D. Nesbit (1871-1927), published in
*Opportunity*, 1914

Who hath a book
Has friends at hand, And gold and gear
At his command; And rich estates,
If he but look, Are held by him
Who hath a book.
Who hath a book
Has but to read, And he may be
A king, indeed; His kingdom is
His inglenook*— All this is his
Who hath a book.


\* a cozy space on each side of a fireplace

# Recommended Winter Picture Books

## Stellar Choices

★Ashby, Ruth. *Caedmon's Song* – Caedmon learns to praise God and write poetry because of what he has experienced of Him in nature.

★Baylor, Byrd. *The Table Where Rich People Sit* – Mountain Girl's poor family count up the value of the things they have. What is the value of the sunrise, the night sky, the smell of coming rain?

★Clark, M. H. *You Belong Here* – With a gentle rhythm and strong connection to the natural world, this book satisfies and soothes like a familiar lullaby.

★Mackall, Dandi. *The Legend of St. Nicholas* – Nick learns the story of St. Nicholas and the true meaning of Christmas and the Christian life.

★Wood, Douglas. *A Quiet Place* – In this gentle book with full-page, peaceful illustrations, Douglas Wood encourages us all to find our own quiet place where we can think our own quiet thoughts.

## Christmas

Berger, Barbara. *The Donkey's Dream* – A donkey dreams that it carries many of the symbols of the Virgin Mary as it carries her and the Christ Child to Bethlehem.

Cole, Joanna. *A Gift from Saint Francis: The First Crèche* – Learn how St. Francis recreated the first Christmas scene in this beautifully illustrated book.

Faber, Norma. *When It Snowed that Night* – Poems about each of the animals and insects that went to Bethlehem that first Christmas morning

Mackall, Dandi. *The Legend of the Christmas Cookie: Sharing the True Meaning of Christmas* – Learn about the origin of baking Christmas cookies, a tradition of giving cookies to others and an important Christmas message.

Mackall, Dandi Daley. *Listen to the Silent Night* – How silent was the night when our dear Savior was born? These short poems center on those who played a role in that first Christmas night.

Mayer, Marianna. *The Real Santa Claus* – This biography of St. Nicolas for older children uses masterpiece paintings and Clement Moore's famous poem to trace the evolution of St. Nick to our current Santa Claus.

McCaughrean, Geraldine. *Father and Son, A Nativity Story* – Sit with St. Joseph near the manger of the newborn King and learn of his joys, his thoughts, and his fears regarding his responsibilities as the foster-father of Jesus. What present can you offer to Jesus in thanksgiving for His many gifts to you?

McCutcheon, John. *Christmas in the Trenches* – Grandfather tells of a Christmas Day he experienced in 1914 during World War I.

Monroe, Colleen. *A Wish to Be a Christmas Tree* – The animals of the forest help the wish of their friend, the towering evergreen, come true in this brightly illustrated Christmas tale.

Moore, Clement. (Tasha Tudor). *The Night before Christmas* – This famous poem is beautifully enhanced with the charming drawings of Tasha Tudor.

Suess, Dr. *How the Grinch Stole Christmas* – In this humorous Christmas classic, the selfless meaning of Christmas shines through the hearts of all in Who-ville.

Westerlund, Kate. *The Message of the Birds* – Little robin insists on sharing the message of Christmas with children as he believes they will listen even when adults may not.

Wilner, Isabel. *B Is for Bethlehem* – A cute Christmas board book, these alphabetic rhymes tell the chronological story of the birth of Jesus.

Wojciechowski, Susan. *The Christmas Miracle of Jonathan Toomey* – Sad Jonathan Toomey accepts a wood-carving job for Christmas that changes his life. The message—with profuse, realistic illustrations—may change yours as well.

Yolen, Jane and Tomie de Paola. *Hark: A Christmas Sampler* – With decorative pages, this book contains many hymns, poems, and stories for Christmas.

## HOLIDAY – GENERAL

dePaola, Tomie. *The Lady of Guadalupe* – For slightly older children, this retelling of the Mexican apparition of our Lady at Guadalupe in 1531 is nicely illustrated.

dePaoli, Tomie. *The Story of the Three Wise Kings* – Simply written with colorful illustrations, this is the story of the Epiphany of the wise men.

Doman, Regina. *Angel in the Waters* – A gentle story of a baby and angel growing from conception to birth, this is an excellent read for the Day of Prayer for the Legal Protection of Unborn Children on January 22.

Spinelli, Eileen. *Somebody Loves You, Mr. Hatch* – Mr. Hatch receives an anonymous valentine. Watch what happens when love—or even the idea of love—catches hold of a person.

Tompert, Ann. *Saint Valentine* – Covering the legends and the facts regarding this saint, the simple text is accompanied with dramatic illustrations and helps us understand what we celebrate, and why, on February 14.

## REFLECTING ON THE MYSTERY OF GOD (MYSTIC)

Baskwill. Jane. *Somewhere* – With sparse, rhyming text and bold illustrations, this book encourages us to take notice of the wonder of daily events in nature.

Florian, Douglas. *Winter Eyes* – This book contains twenty-eight short poems about walking outdoors and listening to winter.

Frost, Robert (Illustrated by Susan Jeffers). *Stopping by Woods on a Snowy Evening* – This is a beautifully illustrated edition of Robert Frost's famous poem.

Hines, Anna Grossnickle. *Sky All Around* – A father and daughter share the wonders of the night sky.

Paulsen, Gary. *Dogteam* – A dogsled team joyously pulls through the winter night in the grandeur of the outdoors.

## DETECTING GOD IN NATURE (NATURE DETECTIVE)

Berenstain, Stan and Jan. *The Berenstain Bear's in the Bears' Almanac: A Year in Bear Country* – Contains information about each of the seasons, holidays, and weather

Borland, Hal. *This World of Wonder* – With the wisdom of a lifelong naturalist, Hal Borland records the marvels of each season, sharing with us the sense of awe and wonder the natural world contains.

George, Jean. *Dear Rebecca, Winter Is Here* – Through a letter to Rebecca, we are shown the overlapping cycles of the seasons.

George, Lindsay Barrett. *In the Snow: Who's Been Here?* – Gorgeous illustrations tell of tracks in the snow and who may have been responsible.

Hader, Berta and Elmer. *The Big Snow* – Beautifully illustrated, this Caldecott Medal book follows the animals of the forest as they get ready for winter.

Lionni, Leo. *Inch by Inch* – This simple story states that all of creation has been given different gifts for different purposes.

Van Laan, Nancy. *When Winter Comes* – Warm and cozy, this book relays simple facts about what happens to animals, fish, and plants when winter comes.

Yolen, Jane. *Sing a Season Song* – With brilliantly clear illustrations, this celebration of the seasons notes attributes of each season as well as the general cycle of time.

# INSPECTING GOD'S GLORIOUS CREATION (NATURALIST)

Arnosky, Jim. *At this Very Moment* – Connects our daily events with those of the animals of the world

Baker, Keith. *No Two Alike* – With adorable pictures and simple text, this book teaches us that all of creation is unique; no two things are quite alike.

Gerber, Carole. *Seeds, Bees, Butterflies and More! Poems for Two Voices* – Brighten your winter by reading these fun, rhyming poems about different nature topics.

Gerber, Carole. *Winter Trees* – Learn to identify trees in winter with this book of bright illustrations and rhyming text.

Zoboli, Giovanna. *I Wish I Had* – Through very simple text and colorful illustrations, we learn about some gifts of the animals, gifts we do not possess. What would it be like to possess these special traits?

## Respecting God's Creation (Eco-Catholic)

Appelt, Kathi. *My Father's House* – Teaching us to be thankful to the Creator, this book covers, in short poems and rich illustrations, many of the world's habitats.

Bruchac, Joseph and Thomas Locker. *Rachel Carson: Preserving a Sense of Wonder* – A short but beautiful and inspiring biography of this first environmentalist

Bunting, Eva. *Night Tree* – In a touching story, Eve Bunting shares a beautiful way to take care of the animals in the woods at Christmas time.

Hopkins, H. Joseph. *The Tree Lady: The True Story of How One Tree-Loving Woman Changed a City Forever* – This short biography of Kate Sessions relates how no one thought so many beautiful varieties of trees could be grown in the desert climate of San Diego, California. But Kate did.

Sams II, Carl R. and Jean Stoick. *A Stranger in the Woods* – A winter "photographic fantasy" that shows how we can creatively care for woodland animals during the coldest months

## GENERAL NATURE BOOKS

Gray, Libba. *My Mama Had a Dancing Heart* – A girl and her mother have a dancing celebration through the seasons.

Hopkins, Lee Bennett. *Sharing the Seasons: A Book of Poems* – In this brightly illustrated book, quotations and poems present winter, spring, summer, and autumn — twelve poems for each season.

Martin, Jacqueline. *Snowflake Bentley* – In this Caldecott Medal book, Wilson Bentley's work in photographing snowflakes is gracefully told and enhanced with lovely woodcuts.

Messner, Kate. *Over and Under the Snow* – Explore the secret kingdom under the snow where animals go to survive the winter.

Rylant, Cynthia. *long night moon* – Short, poetic text with accompanying pictures of the Native American full moons

Schnur, Steven. *Winter: An Alphabet Acrostic* – Nicely illustrated, the highlights of winter are presented in poetic acrostics.

Sendak, Maurice. *Chicken Soup with Rice: A Book of Months* – Although a book about months rather than seasons, this classic book deserves to be included in the recommended list—a family favorite!

Stevenson, Robert L. and Brian Wildsmith. *A Child's Garden of Verses* – Brian Wildsmith's artwork is the backdrop for the poetry of Robert Lewis Stevenson.

Teckentrup, Britta. *Tree* – What an engaging way to illustrate the seasonal changes of a tree and its forest companions for young children!

Tripp, Nathaniel. *Snow Comes to the Farm* – With beautiful, realistic paintings, this is a story of brotherly love and nature-sharing while awaiting the first snowstorm of the season.

Yolen, Jane. *Owl Moon* – Winner of the Caldecott Medal, *Owl Moon* uses winter watercolors and gentle text to tell the story of a girl and her father who go out owling when the winter moon is full.

## Children's Nature Non-Fiction Books

Listed below is a short list of reference books on various aspects of nature.

*Nature Anatomy: The Curious Parts & Pieces of the Natural World* by Julia Rothman

*WoodWalk: Peepers, Porcupines, & Exploding Puffballs!* by Henry W. Art and Michael W. Robbins

*Stick Book (The), Loads of Things You Can Make or Do with a Stick* by Fiona Danks and Jo Schofield

*Wild Weather Book: Loads of Things to Do Outdoors in Rain, Wind, and Snow* by Fiona Danks

# RECOMMENDED ADULT RESOURCES

The following lists of books are intended to aid you in becoming more confident as a nature mentor and student of natural history. This subject used to be taught in schools along with reading, writing, and 'rithmetic. In addition, years ago people were more connected to nature through farming, gardening, and general rural living. Scott Sampson states, "By the close of the 1900s, most Americans could describe themselves as naturalists" (*How to Raise a Wild Child*). Browse through the lists and pick at least one book from each category to educate and inspire you. Most books can be found in your local library or purchased new or used online.

The "Why" of Nature

- 📖 *Last Child in the Woods: Saving Our Children from Nature-Deficit Disorder* by Richard Louv
- 📖 *Step into Nature: Nurturing Imagination and Spirit in Everyday Life* by Patrice Vecchione
- 📖 *The Joyful Mystery: Field Notes toward a Green Thomism* by Christopher J. Thompson
- 📖 *The Nature Fix: Why Nature Makes Us Happier, Healthier, and More Creative* by Florence Williams

Connection with Nature

- 📖 *A Blessing of Toads: A Guide to Living with Nature* by Sharon Lovejoy
- 📖 *How to Be a Wildflower: A Field Guide* by Katie Daisy
- 📖 *The Curious Nature Guide: Explore the Natural Wonders All Around You* by Clare Walker Leslie
- 📖 *The Secret Wisdom of Nature: Trees, Animals, and the Extraordinary Balance of All Living Things* by Peter Wohlleben

📖 *What the Robin Knows: How Birds Reveal the Secrets of the Natural World* by Jon Young

Nature Activity Books—Outdoor Adventuring

📖 *15 Minutes Outside: 365 Ways to Get Out of the House and Connect with Your Kids* by Rebecca P. Cohen [elementary age]

📖 *Go Wild! 101 Things to Do Outdoors before You Grow Up* by Jo Schofield and Fiona Danks [teens]

📖 *Hands-On Nature: Information and Activities for Exploring the Environment with Children* by Jenepher Lingelbach [Grades K-6]

📖 *I Love Dirt: 52 Activities to Help You and Your Kids Discover the Wonders of Nature* by Jennifer Ward [ages 4-8]

📖 *Roots, Shoots, Buckets & Boots: Gardening Together with Children* by Sharon Lovejoy

📖 *Teaching Kids to Love the Earth: Sharing a Sense of Wonder . . . 186 Outdoor Activities for Parents and Other Teachers* by Herman, Passineau, Schimpf, & Treuer [all ages]

📖 *The Boy's Book of Adventure: The Little Guidebook for Smart and Resourceful Boys* by Michele Lecreux [for girls too!]

📖 *The Wild Weather Book: Loads of Things to Do Outdoors in Rain, Wind and Snow* by Fiona Danks and Jo Schofield

📖 *Vitamin N: The Essential Guide to a Nature-Rich Life—500 Ways to Enrich the Health & Happiness of Your Family & Community* by Richard Louv

Nature Journaling

📖 *Drawn to Nature through the Journals of Clare Walker Leslie*

  📖 *Keeping a Nature Journal: Discover a Whole New Way of Seeing the World Around You* by Clare Walker Leslie & Charles E. Roth [ideas and "how to"]

  📖 *Nature Journal: A Guided Journal for Illustrating and Recording Your Observations of the Natural World* with Clare Walker Leslie

  📖 *The Country Diary of an Edwardian Lady* by Edith Holden

  📖 *The Naturalist's Notebook for Tracking Changes in the Natural World Around You* by Nathaniel T. Wheelwright & Bernd Heinrich

Nature Crafts and Drawing Books

  📖 *Crafting with Nature: Grow or Gather Your Own Supplies for Simple Handmade Crafts, Gifts & Recipes* by Amy Renea

  📖 *Make It Wild: 101 Things to Make and Do Outdoors* by Fiona Danks and Jo Schofield

  📖 *Nature Crafts for Kids: 50 Fantastic Things to Make with Mother Nature's Help* by Gwen Diehn & Terry Krautwurst

  📖 *Peggy Dean's Guide to Nature Drawing and Watercolor: Learn to Sketch, Ink, and Paint Flowers, Plants, Trees, and Animals* by Peggy Dean

Nature Books for Grandparents

  📖 *Granny Camp by Sharon Lovejoy*

  📖 *The Rhythm of Family: Discovering a Sense of Wonder through the Seasons* by Amanda Blake Soule with Stephen Soule

  📖 *Toad Cottages & Shooting Stars: Grandma's Bag of Tricks* by Sharon Lovejoy

The Practice of *Shinrin-yoku:* Forest Therapy or Forest Bathing

    📖 *Your Guide to Forest Bathing: Experience the Healing Power of Nature* by M. Amos Clifford

    📖 Review the teaching philosophies of educators such as Maria Montessori and Charlotte Mason

The Practice of Mindfulness

    📖 *A Catholic Guide to Mindfulness* by Susan Brinkmann, OCDS

    📖 *The Mindful Catholic: Finding God One Moment at a Time* by Dr Gregory Bottaro

    📖 *The Practice of the Presence of God* by Br. Lawrence of the Resurrection

    📖 *The Sacrament of the Present Moment* by Jean-Pierre de Caussade (also published as *Abandonment to Divine Providence*)

> "For if they so far succeeded in knowledge that they could speculate about the world, how did they not more quickly find its Lord?"
>
> Wisdom 13:9

# APPENDIX

# SEEKING GOD IN NATURE
## WITH THE CHURCH

# ASSURANCES AND GENERAL COUNSELS: SEEKING GOD IN NATURE VS. NATURE WORSHIP

With the advent of the New Age Movement or New Age Spirituality, many Catholics have become rightfully cautious regarding seeking God (and praying with Him) in nature as this book series promotes. In order to reassure you and provide some general counsel and advice, the following "lessons" are provided regarding the proper place the reverence of God has in His creation and the appropriateness of communing with Him in the natural world. Below are various appropriate passages from the *Catechism of the Catholic Church*, papal documents, and teachings of the United States bishops. By following the guidelines established with these various Church authorities, we can be assured not to go astray or to lead others down a questionable path of holiness.

Remember these basic principles when using the natural world to converse with God and advance in the life of prayer:

1. God is distinct from His creation. A tree is not God, but can help us better understand the attributes, love, and mercy of God.

2. While it is our intent to learn more about the natural world, this knowledge is for the sole purpose of uniting ourselves closer to the living God, the God of all creation.

3. There is nothing that exists that was not created by God—with a purpose. By understanding the uniqueness of each individual creation, its God-given purpose, and its connection to the rest of

creation, we can learn much about God and our relationship with Him and His creation.

4. God wants you to be surrounded with truth, beauty, and goodness. Creation gives us a glimpse of these features of God and fills us with gratitude.

5. The sole purpose of our existence is to unite our will perfectly with the Will of God and so attain perfect happiness in heaven. Any thing, any person, or any "method" or means of prayer that impedes our goal of uniting ourselves with the Triune God by increasing our self-centeredness or deflecting the reverence that belongs to God to any other person or object is not in accordance with divine teaching or the authority of the Catholic Church.

I promote communing with God in the natural world as it has worked unfailingly for me throughout my life—even as a professed Secular Carmelite. God speaks in eternal silence and in holy silence must be heard by the soul. This silence is often found in the stillness of the natural world. Matthew Kelly often speaks of spending time in the "classroom of silence." For me, nature provides the best classroom—free of the distractions of daily life.

If I spend too little time in silence with God in nature, my peace quickly evaporates, just as not frequenting the sacraments or spending too little time with Jesus in the Blessed Sacrament of the Altar does.

What drew me as a convert to the Catholic Church is the Church's vast array of available means to attain holiness. Perhaps this method of communing with the God of the universe will assist you—and your loved ones as well—along the path of holiness. That is my deep desire.

# A BRIEF LESSON ON NEW AGE SPIRITUALITY

While the gamut of New Age spirituality is vast and is composed of a variety of theologies, consider the following generally accepted principles of this philosophy: (Note that all of these are in conflict with the teachings of the Catholic Church.)

- No central authority or teaching, no formal doctrine, or membership
- Contains part of many "isms" such as Pantheism (All things are divine.), Gnosticism (salvation by knowledge), and occultism (knowledge or use of supernatural forces or beings)
- God and creation are one. There is no separation between them.
- Christ is a type of energy, not necessarily an individual being.
- Morality is individually determined—moral relativism
- Influenced by Eastern religions and forms of meditation
- Man is divine and perfected through reincarnation.

For our purposes, remember that God and creation are not one. Creation is a *reflection* of God and can help us come to know Him better. Knowledge of the natural world serves to draw us into closer union with the Creator as we come to see the diversity, beauty, and goodness of nature. We can become more deeply connected to God —and grow in gratitude for His constant presence and many gifts—when we see His hand in the world around us and can pray gratefully to Him in the silence of creation. We can join with all creation to sing praise to the glory of our loving God!

# LESSONS FROM THE *CATECHISM OF THE CATHOLIC CHURCH*

The following are excerpts from the *Catechism* regarding God and the natural (visible) world that should assure us that this path of union with God is trustworthy and in full communion with the Holy See:

¶32 . . . As St. Paul says of the Gentiles: For what can be known about God is plain to them, because God has shown it to them. Ever since the creation of the world his invisible nature, namely, his eternal power and deity, has been clearly perceived in the things that have been made (Rom 1:19-20; cf., Acts 14:15, 17; 17:27-28; Wis 13:1-9). And St. Augustine issues this challenge: Question the beauty of the earth, question the beauty of the sea, question the beauty of the air distending and diffusing itself, question the beauty of the sky . . . question all these realities. All respond: "See, we are beautiful." Their beauty is a profession [*confessio*]. These beauties are subject to change. Who made them if not the Beautiful One [Pulcher] who is not subject to change? (St. Augustine, *Sermo* 241, 2: Patrologia Latina 38, 1134)

¶41 All creatures bear a certain resemblance to God, most especially man, created in the image and likeness of God. The manifold perfections of creatures—their truth, their goodness, their beauty all reflect the infinite perfection of God. Consequently we can name God by taking his creatures' perfections as our starting point, "for from the greatness and beauty of created things comes a corresponding perception of their Creator" (Wisdom 13:5).

¶293 Scripture and Tradition never cease to teach and celebrate this fundamental truth: "The world was made for the glory of God" (*Dei Filius*, can. # 5: S 3025). St. Bonaventure explains that God created all things "not to increase his glory, but to show it forth and to communicate it" (St. Bonaventure, *In II Sent.* I, 2, 2, 1), for God has no other reason for creating than his love and goodness: "Creatures came into existence when the key of love opened his hand" (St. Thomas Aquinas, *Sent. II*, prol.). The First Vatican Council explains:

This one, true God, of his own goodness and "almighty power", not for increasing his own beatitude, nor for attaining his perfection, but in order to manifest this perfection through the benefits which he bestows on creatures, with absolute freedom of counsel "and from the beginning of time, made out of nothing both orders of creatures, the spiritual and the corporeal. . ." (13 *Dei Filius* I: DS 3002; cf Lateran Council IV (1215): DS 800.7)

¶294 The glory of God consists in the realization of this manifestation and communication of his goodness, for which the world was created. . . ."

GOD TRANSCENDS CREATION AND IS PRESENT TO IT
¶300 God is infinitely greater than all his works: "You have set your glory above the heavens" (Ps 8:1; cf. Sir 43:28). Indeed, God's "greatness is unsearchable" (Ps 145:3). But because he is the free and sovereign Creator, the first cause of all that exists, God is present to his creatures' inmost being: "In him we live and move and have our being" (Acts 17:28). In the words of St. Augustine, God is "higher than my highest and more inward than my innermost self" (St. Augustine, Conf: 3, 6, 11: PL 32, 688). God upholds and sustains creation.

¶337 God himself created the visible world in all its richness, diversity and order. . . . On the subject of creation, the sacred text teaches the truths revealed by God for our salvation (*Dei Verbum* Cf. 11), permitting us to "recognize the inner nature, the value and the ordering of the whole of creation to the praise of God" (*Lumen Gentium* 36 #2).

¶338 Nothing exists that does not owe its existence to God the Creator. . . .

¶339 Each creature possesses its own particular goodness and perfection. . . . Each of the various creatures, willed in its own being, reflects in its own way a ray of God's infinite wisdom and goodness. Man must therefore respect the particular goodness of every creature, to avoid any disordered use of things which would be in contempt of the Creator and would bring disastrous consequences for human beings and their environment.

¶340 God wills the interdependence of creatures: the sun and the moon, the cedar and the little flower, the eagle and the sparrow: the spectacle of their countless diversities and inequalities tells us that no creature is self-sufficient. Creatures exist only in dependence on each other, to complete each other, in the service of each other.

¶341 The beauty of the universe: the order and harmony of the created world results from the diversity of beings and from the relationships which exist among them. Man discovers them progressively as the laws of nature. They call forth the admiration of scholars. The beauty of creation reflects the infinite beauty of the Creator and ought to inspire the respect and submission of man's intellect and will.

¶344 There is a solidarity among all creatures arising from the fact that all have the same Creator and are all ordered to his glory . . .

¶2416 *Animals* are God's creatures. He surrounds them with his providential care. By their mere existence they bless him and give him glory (Cf. Mt 6:26; Dan 3:79-81). Thus men owe them kindness. We should recall the gentleness with which saints like St. Francis of Assisi or St. Philip Neri treated animals.

## LESSONS FROM RECENT PAPAL DOCUMENTS

One of the earliest papal documents to call attention to the environment is Pope Saint Paul VI's 1971 letter, *Octogesima Adveniens*, his reflection on the challenges of the post-industrial society. Here, he calls the environment a "wide-ranging social problem which concerns the entire human family" (¶21). Pope Saint John Paul II again addresses ecological matters in the 1988 *Sollicitudo Socialis (On Social Concern)*; and, in 1990, became the first pope to devote an entire papal document to the environmental issue: "Peace with God the Creator, Peace with All of Creation" (1990)—a document well worth reading. An entire chapter of *The Compendium of the Social Doctrine of the Church* (2004) addresses the topic of "Safeguarding the Environment." This chapter was condensed into "The Ten Commandments for the Environment" by Bishop Giampaolo Crepaldi in 2005.

Pope Benedict XVI spent so much of his papacy promoting an environmental message through addresses, encyclicals, and scientific conferences that he became known as the "Green Pope." Pope Francis has spoken frequently about ecological concerns and addressed his 2015 encyclical *Laudato Si': On Care for Our Common*

*Home* not just to a Catholic audience but to "every person living on this planet" (¶3).

For our purposes, however, let us limit our study to those papal references that especially address seeking and praising God in creation.

"PEACE WITH GOD THE CREATOR, PEACE WITH ALL OF CREATION" (Pope Saint John Paul II, 1990):

¶13 An education in ecological responsibility is urgent . . . The first educator, however, is the family, where the child learns to respect his neighbor and to love nature.

¶14 Finally, the aesthetic value of creation cannot be overlooked. Our very contact with nature has a deep restorative power; contemplation of its magnificence imparts peace and serenity. The Bible speaks again and again of the goodness and beauty of creation, which is called to glorify God . . .

¶16 It is my hope that the inspiration of Saint Francis will help us to keep ever alive a sense of "fraternity" with all those good and beautiful things which Almighty God has created. And may he remind us of our serious obligation to respect and watch over them with care, in light of that greater and higher fraternity that exists within the human family.

*COMPENDIUM OF THE SOCIAL DOCTRINE OF THE CHURCH* (2004):

*¶487 The attitude that must characterize the way man acts in relation to creation is essentially one of gratitude and appreciation; the world, in fact, reveals the mystery of God who created and sustains it.* If the relationship with God is placed aside, nature is stripped of its profound meaning and impoverished. If on the other hand,

nature is rediscovered in its creaturely dimension, channels of communication with it can be established, its rich and symbolic meaning can be understood, allowing us to enter into its realm of *mystery*. This realm opens the path of man to God, Creator of heaven and earth. *The world presents itself before man's eyes as evidence of God*, the place where his creative, providential and redemptive power unfolds.

*CARITAS IN VERITATE* (Pope Benedict XVI, 2009): ¶48 ". . . Nature speaks to us of the Creator (cf. Romans 1:20) and his love for humanity."

MEETING WITH PRIESTS AND DEACONS—August 6, 2008, Pope Benedict XVI: "If we observe what came into being around monasteries, how in those places small paradises, oases of creation were and continue to be born, it becomes evident that these were not only words. Rather, wherever the Creator's Word was properly understood, wherever life was lived with the redeeming Creator, people strove to save creation and not to destroy it."

*LAUDATO SI'* (Pope Francis, 2015):

¶85 "From panoramic vistas to the tiniest living form, nature is a constant source of wonder and awe. It is also a continuing revelation of the divine." . . . "To sense each creature singing the hymn of its existence is to live joyfully in God's love and hope." This contemplation of creation allows us to discover in each thing a teaching which God wishes to hand on to us, "for the believer, to contemplate creation is the hear a message, to listen to a paradoxical and silent voice."

¶87 When we can see God reflected in all that exists, our hearts are moved to praise the Lord for all his creatures and to worship him in union with them.

¶97 As he [Jesus] made his way throughout the land, he often stopped to contemplate the beauty sown by his Father, and invited his disciples to perceive a divine message in things . . .

¶233 The universe unfolds in God, who fills it completely. Hence, there is a mystical meaning to be found in a leaf, in a mountain trail, in a dewdrop, in a poor person's face. The ideal is not only to pass from the exterior to the interior to discover the action of God in the soul, but also to discover God in all things.

¶234 ". . . the mystic experiences the intimate connection between God and all beings, and thus feels that all things are God." Standing awestruck before a mountain, he or she cannot separate this experience from God, and perceives that the interior awe being lived has to be entrusted to the Lord . . .

¶246 . . . Teach us to discover the worth of each thing, to be filled with awe and contemplation, to recognize that we are profoundly united with every creature as we journey towards your infinite light.

## LESSONS FROM THE UNITED STATES CONFERENCE OF CATHOLIC BISHOPS

In 1991, the United States Conference of Catholic Bishops published *Renewing the Earth: An Invitation to Reflection and Action on Environment in Light of Catholic Social Teaching,* and, in 2001, *Global Climate Change: A Plea for Dialogue, Prudence, and the Common Good.* Let us examine some excerpts from the former document.

For many people, the environmental movement has reawakened appreciation of the truth that, through the created gifts of nature, men and women encounter their

Creator. The Christian vision of a sacramental universe —a world that discloses the Creator's presence by visible and tangible signs—can contribute to making the earth a home for the human family once again. Pope John Paul II has called for Christians to respect and protect the environment, so that through nature people can "contemplate the mystery of the greatness and love of God. . . . Dwelling in the presence of God, we begin to experience ourselves as part of creation, as stewards within it, not separate from it. As faithful stewards, fullness of life comes from living responsibly within God's creation (III-A).

Nature shares in God's goodness, and contemplation of its beauty and richness raised our hearts and minds to God. . . . Through the centuries, Catholic theologians and philosophers, like St. Paul before them, continue to search for God in reasoning about the created world (IV-A).

We remind *parents* that they are the first and principal teachers of children. It is from parents that children will learn love of the earth and delight in nature. It is at home that they develop the habits of self-control, concern, and care that lie at the heart of environmental morality (V-B).

## Two Current Practices

Seeking God and communing with Him in nature raises several potential "red flags" regarding two currently popular practices: the Japanese practice of *shinrin-yoka*, or forest therapy (forest bathing) and mindfulness.

Many scientific studies show that spending time in nature can have a positive effect on us physically, emotionally, and spiritually. Forest therapy, a concept practiced instinctively for eons, has fallen from practice in modern times. Spending refreshing periods of time with God in the natural world can be spiritually empowering. Organized "immersions" are becoming popular. Be cautious and aware, ensuring that the focus centers on God the Creator—source of all existence.

Mindfulness, derived from a Buddhist meditation technique, also has the potential to lead a Catholic astray. Although similar to the accepted Catholic practices of the Practice of the Presence of God and the Sacrament of the Present Moment, Buddhist mindfulness is centered on the mind; Catholic meditation always centers on God. We want to treasure each moment with God in the natural world, but only in a way that leads us directly to Him.

Educate yourself regarding these two practices by reading one or more of the resources suggested in the Appendix, or research these practices online.

---

As we deepen our connection with nature—and therefore with our loving God—let us try to develop a "sacramental imagination." According to Mary C. Boys, this is a "vision that sees all creation as mediating the divine." This vision may be easier for children than adults. To seek God through His creation, search for His reflection —consider what each creation can teach us about God, and embrace each gift of nature as a continuation of the mystery that is God: "Even when he reveals himself, God remains a mystery beyond words: 'If you understood him, it would not be God'" *(CCC* ¶230 quoting St. Augustine).

Immerse yourself in nature. Ponder in holy silence His wondrous creation. In all things, give Him glory. Give thanks.